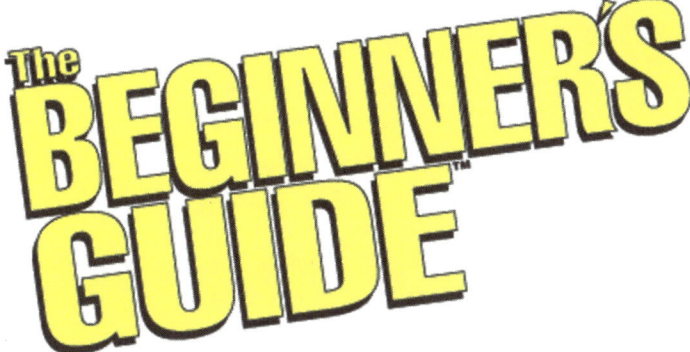

The BEGINNER'S GUIDE

Everything you need to learn and use

MS WORD 97

OUR MISSION

Students, supervisors, employees and users seldom use all the features available in their software. What most people need to know is how to perform specific tasks quickly and easily. They need the ability to painlessly write a letter, report, budget, or set up a mailing list. The Beginner's Guide uses everyday examples to guide readers step-by-step through the commands they will use the most. Clear, understandable lessons combined with concise illustrations provide the information you need to learn and understand most software and features used in everyday tasks.

ACCESS Publishing is committed to providing proven solutions that let you easily and quickly learn your software. Established in 1989, ACCESS Publishing offers high quality software training products that reflect the company's unique understanding of the new ways in which individuals and businesses must work together to achieve success. ACCESS Publishing's innovative approach is evident in a class of training guides that allows you to access information in easy to understand terms.

A Personal Workstations, Inc. Company
3015 112th Avenue NE Suite 205, Bellevue, WA 98004
Printed in the U.S.A.

The BEGINNER'S GUIDE MS Word 97
Published by ACCESS Publishing, a subsidiary of Personal Workstations, Inc.

No part of this publication may be reproduced, stored in a retrieval system or transmitted in any form or by any means, electronic or mechanical, including photocopying, recording or otherwise, for any purpose without the express written permission of Access Publishing Inc.

ISBN 1-57671-013-0

Cover Design by
Shaun Wolden Design

Acknowledgements
Special thanks to Heidi Steele for her contributions in making this book possible. Heidi Steele is a freelance writer, computer trainer, and editor of major computer publications.

Table of Contents

Microsoft Word 97

Table of Contents

Working with Long Documents

Styles

Templates and Wizards

Columns and Tables

Mail Merge

How to Use This Book

Guaranteed the fastest and easiest way to learn new software

This book is designed to help you become software proficient in the shortest possible time. Each turned page is a complete lesson, written in easy to understand, non-technical terms. Each lesson includes step-by-step instructions, practical examples, and clear illustrations. The instructions avoid computer jargon and lead the reader from simple tasks to advanced techniques. The examples and illustrations are based on practical "real world" tasks performed by most users.

How The BEGINNER'S GUIDE is organized

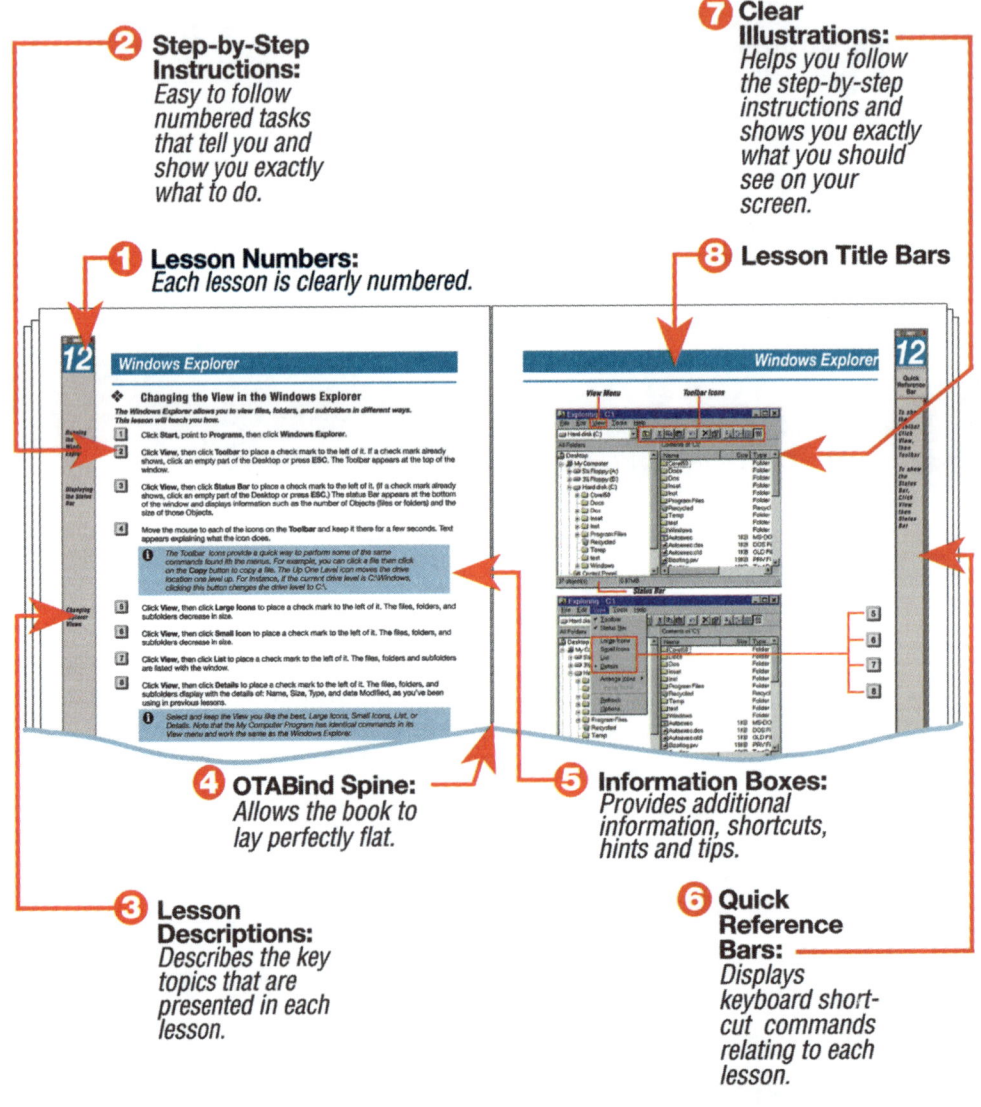

7 Clear Illustrations:
Helps you follow the step-by-step instructions and shows you exactly what you should see on your screen.

2 Step-by-Step Instructions:
Easy to follow numbered tasks that tell you and show you exactly what to do.

1 Lesson Numbers:
Each lesson is clearly numbered.

8 Lesson Title Bars

4 OTABind Spine:
Allows the book to lay perfectly flat.

5 Information Boxes:
Provides additional information, shortcuts, hints and tips.

3 Lesson Descriptions:
Describes the key topics that are presented in each lesson.

6 Quick Reference Bars:
Displays keyboard short-cut commands relating to each lesson.

 Always make sure the power is disconnected before removing the computer cover or any of the components.

Your Personal Computer

1 When you set up your system, it's important to consider location. Your computer must have room for proper air circulation so that it doesn't overheat. Don't put the computer in an enclosed cabinet or close to a wall.

 Once your computer is set up, never unplug a cable or power cord while the computer is running. You could lose important data or damage your computer's components. You should also protect your PC from power fluctuations by plugging all power cords into a surge protector.

2 Your PC is made up of a collection of various components that interact together as one unit. The essential parts of your PC are:

CPU
Monitor
Keyboard
Mouse
Printer

3 Disk drives are used to store software programs and data files. The three types of disk drives are *floppy disk drives*, *hard disk drives*, and *CD-ROM disk drives*. Floppy disk drives store data on removable 3 ˝-inch disks. Hard disk drives are usually mounted inside of the PC. The hard disk is fixed permanently inside of the drive. CD-ROM disk drives read information from removable CD-ROM disks; these drives are read-only.

4 Software programs send instructions to different parts of the computer through a special set of programs called an *operating system*. The operating system is responsible for starting the computer, loading application programs, and controlling the PC's keyboard, monitor, printer, ports, and disk drives. Windows 95, the operating system required to run Microsoft Office 97, is usually preinstalled on your hard disk by the manufacturer.

5 The startup cycle that occurs when you turn on your PC is called *booting up*. During the boot process, your PC loads portions of the operating system into Random Access Memory (RAM). The initial boot process is called a *cold boot*. Restarting your computer when it is turned on (by clicking the Start button, clicking Shut Down, clicking the Restart the Computer option button, and clicking OK) is called a *warm boot*.

Your Personal Computer

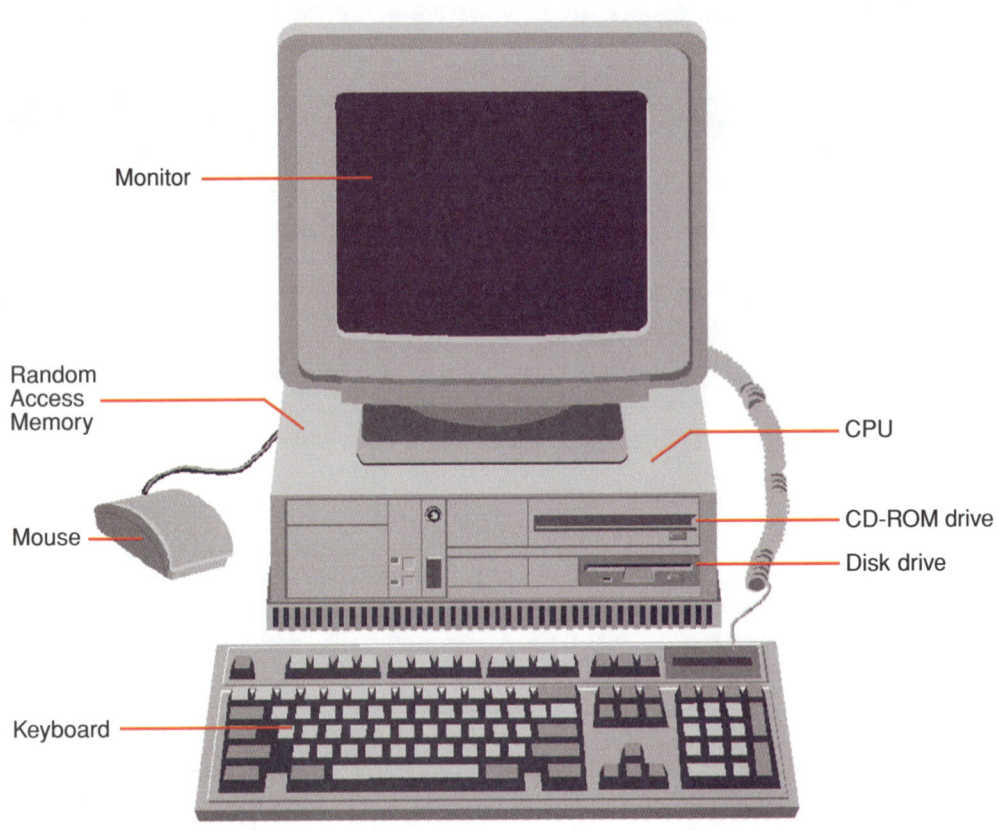

Monitor

Random Access Memory

Mouse

Keyboard

CPU

CD-ROM drive

Disk drive

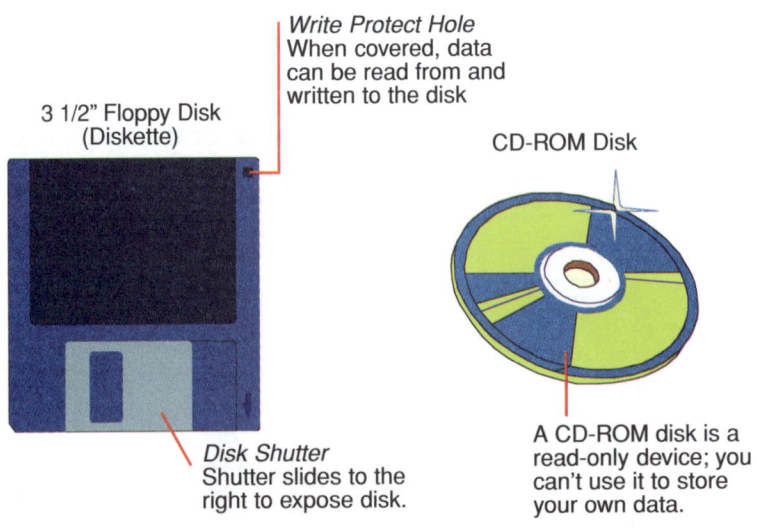

3 1/2" Floppy Disk (Diskette)

Write Protect Hole
When covered, data can be read from and written to the disk

CD-ROM Disk

Disk Shutter
Shutter slides to the right to expose disk.

A CD-ROM disk is a read-only device; you can't use it to store your own data.

 Floppy Disk Storage Tip
Keep floppy disks away from magnets and home appliances such as telephones, stereos, and televisions.

Your Personal Computer

1 *Random access memory (RAM)* is the computer's primary working memory. Your computer stores program instructions and data in RAM to make them accessible directly to the CPU. It is important to remember that RAM only works when the computer is turned on.

2 The *motherboard* is the main circuit board in your PC. Many other components are mounted on the motherboard.

3 The *CPU,* short for *Central Processing Unit* (also called the *microprocessor*), is your PC's most important component. It does all your PC's thinking and runs all of your application programs. The CPU is a chip on the motherboard.

4 The *power supply* provides all the computer components with the correct power voltages. It converts your high-voltage current into the required low-voltage current.

5 *Read Only Memory (ROM)* contains instructions that the computer uses for processes such as booting up. These instructions are written on the ROM chip during manufacturing, and they are permanent. In other words, they remain on the ROM chip even when your PC is turned off.

6 The *video card* takes all the stored memory images generated by your PC and links them to the monitor for display.

7 The *disk drive controller card* controls your PC's disk drives and transfers data. Sometimes the disk drive controller is part of the motherboard itself.

8 The *battery* powers a clock that keeps track of time when the computer is turned off. It also maintains low-voltage electricity for certain RAM chips that have a record of what components are installed in your system.

9 *Ports* are entry/exit boundary mechanisms that govern and synchronize the flow of data between the CPU from and to external devices such as printers and modems.

10 The *floppy disk drive* consists of a slot to accept a floppy disk, a motor that spins the disk and a reading/writing device that moves across the disk to read and write data.

11 The *hard disk drive* is the main permanent storage unit. It contains a hard disk (the disk is actually made up of several platters) that can contain large amounts of data and programs. The data on your hard drive is not affected when you turn off the PC; it remains there unless you overwrite it or the hard disk is damaged.

12 The *CD-ROM drive* is like the floppy disk drive, but it plays CD-ROM disks. CD-ROM drives can only read data from a disk, although some newer ones, called *CD-R drives*, allow you to write data to a disk as well.

 Your PC is best left undisturbed, but if you must open the case, remember to disconnect it from the power source.

System Requirements

MS Word 97 requires the following software and hardware components:

Operating System – Microsoft Windows 95 or Microsoft Windows NT. Windows 95 and Windows NTdo not require DOS. However, they do include a version of DOS in case you need to run old DOS programs.

Microprocessor – Minimum 80486 DX

Memory – Minimum 8MB

Hard Disk Space – Minimum 40MB available

Video Adapter – Enhanced graphics adapter (EGA) or better

Pointing Device – Microsoft mouse or compatible

 If you use a virus protection program, make sure to turn it off before you run the setup program to install Word 97.

Assumptions

The Beginner's Guides are designed to help business people quickly master the leading software programs. Working through the lessons in this guide will get you up and running in MS Word 97 in the shortest possible time.

Assumptions

This guide assumes that you are familiar with Windows 95, and that you are using a Microsoft-compatible mouse, trackball, or other pointing device.

This is not a typical tutorial. We have kept data entry to a minimum so that you can focus on acquiring skills and learning concepts instead of typing.

Conventions

MS Word 97 allows you to issue commands with both the mouse and the keyboard.

Keyboard shortcuts are included throughout the book. Some of these shortcuts require that you press two keys simultaneously. If, for example, you are asked to "press Ctrl+F10," then you should hold down the Ctrl key as you press F10, and then release both keys.

Menu commands are written with a comma separating the menu name from the command. For example, "choose File, Open" means click File in the menu bar to display the File menu, and then click the Open command in the menu.

Text you should type at the keyboard is displayed in boldface. For example, an instruction might tell you to "click in the File Name text box, type **My Practice File**, and click the OK button."

 Information boxes provide additional guidance and helpful tips.

MS WORD 97

Getting Started

❖ A Tour of the Word Window

In this lesson, you learn the basic elements of the Word window.

1 Start Word by clicking the Start button, pointing to Programs, and clicking Microsoft Word.

2 At the top of the Word window is the *title bar*, which tells you the name of the application (Microsoft Word) and the name of the document (Document1). Inside of the Word window (also called the *application window*) is the *document window*, which contains the text area where you type your document. By default, the document window is *maximized*, meaning that it fills the whole Word window. In this state, the document shares the title bar with the application, as shown in the figure on the facing page. If, however, the document window is *restored* (reduced to a smaller size), the document window gets its own separate title bar.

3 Directly beneath the title bar is the menu bar. To pull down a menu, click the menu name. You can then issue a command in the menu by clicking it. To hide a menu that's currently displayed without choosing a command, click anywhere outside of the menu in the text area. To display a menu with the keyboard, press the Alt key and the underlined letter in the menu name. For example, press Alt+T to pull down the Tools menu, or Alt+O to pull down the Format menu. Once a menu is displayed, you can issue a command in the menu by pressing its underlined letter. To hide a menu, press the Alt key.

4 The three buttons at the right end of the title bar control the application window. The corresponding set of buttons at the right end of the menu bar control the document window. The Minimize button for the application hides the window and leaves its button on the Windows 95 taskbar. (To redisplay the window, click the taskbar button.) The Minimize button for the document shrinks the window to a button at the bottom of the application window. (To redisplay the window, click the button.) The Maximize button for the application makes the window fill the screen. The Maximize button for the document makes the window fill the application window. When a window is maximized, the Maximize button automatically becomes a Restore button, which you can click to restore the window to its former size. The Close buttons (also called *Close boxes*) close the application or document window.

5 The Standard toolbar contains shortcuts for basic commands such as Open, Save, Print, and Undo. The Formatting toolbar contains shortcuts for commands that change the appearance of the document. The ruler lets you set tabs and indents, and it shows you where the margins are. Depending on the current view, you can use the ruler to change the margins as well. (If you don't see the ruler, choose View, Ruler to display it.) The status bar tells you what page you're on, the total number of pages, and where your insertion point is on the page.

6 The Browse buttons in the lower-right corner of the document window let you quickly jump from one part of your document to the next. The View buttons let you change the way your document is displayed on screen. You'll learn more about them in "Switching Views and Zooming" later in this book.

7 Click the upper Close box to close Word. (You can also choose File, Exit, or press Alt+F4.)

Getting Started

Quick
Reference
Bar

Press
Alt+F4 to
exit Word

Title bar

Menu bar

Standard
toolbar

Control
buttons

Formatting
toolbar

Ruler

Text area

Vertical
scroll bar

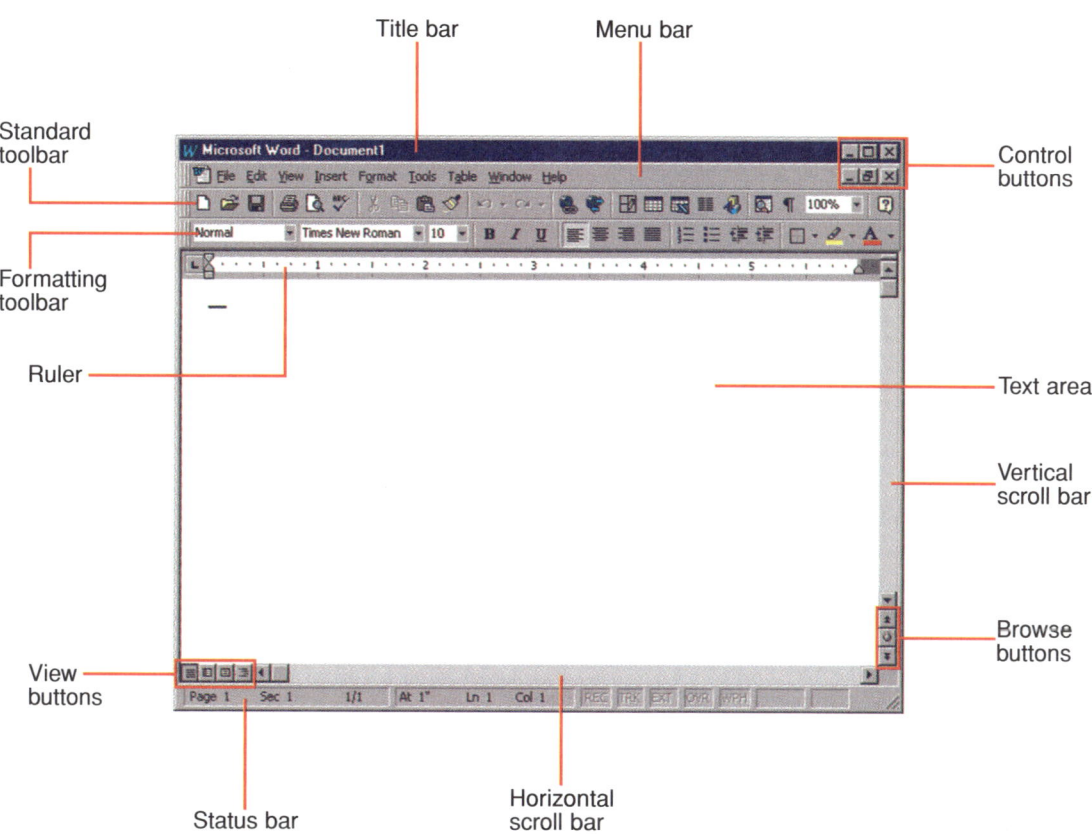

Browse
buttons

View
buttons

Status bar

Horizontal
scroll bar

Minimize

Maximize

Restore

Close

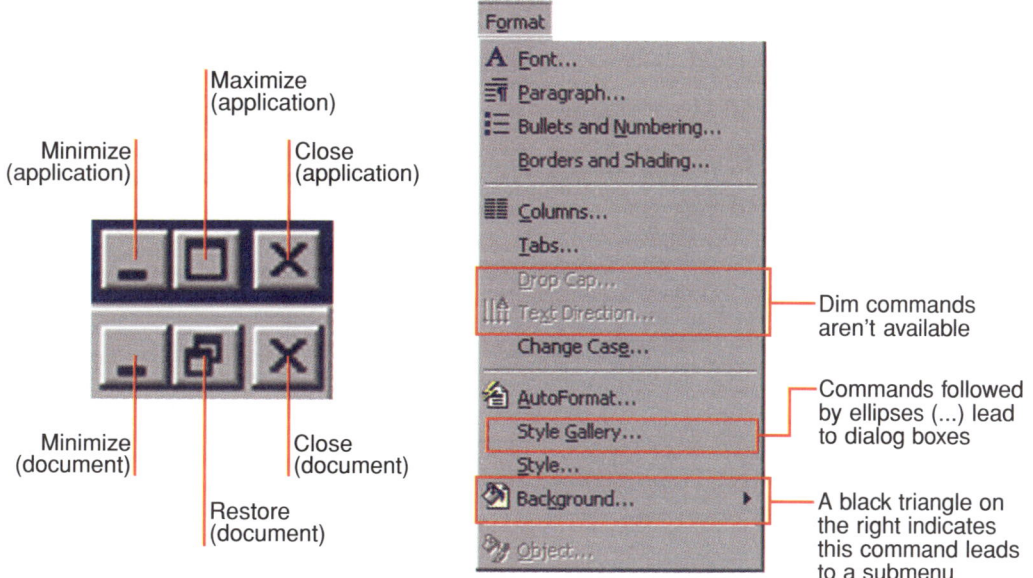

Minimize
(application)

Maximize
(application)

Close
(application)

Minimize
(document)

Restore
(document)

Close
(document)

Dim commands
aren't available

Commands followed
by ellipses (...) lead
to dialog boxes

A black triangle on
the right indicates
this command leads
to a submenu

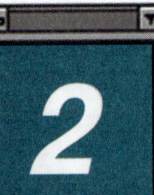

Getting Started

❖ **Customizing Word**

When you install Microsoft Office, Word is configured with default settings. In this lesson, you change two of these settings to get ready to follow the lessons in the remainder of this book. First, you change the default font size from 10 point to 12 point. (A 12-point font is standard for most business documents.) Second, you tell Word your own name and address. Word uses this information whenever it automatically enters your return address in a document such as an envelope or a fax cover sheet.

Changing the default font size

1 Start Word, and choose Format, Font to display the Font dialog box.

2 Click the Font tab if it isn't already in front. In the Font list, choose Times New Roman. In the Font Style list, choose Regular. In the Size list, choose 12. Make sure that Underline is set to None, Color is set to Auto, and none of the check boxes under Effects are marked. Click the Default button.

3 Word displays a message box confirming that you want to set the default font to Times New Roman, 12 point, and it reminds you that this change will affect all documents you create that are based on the Normal template. (You'll learn more about templates in "Creating a Fax Cover Sheet Using a Template" later in this book.) Click Yes, and then click OK to close the Font dialog box.

Now whenever you start a new document in Word, the font will automatically be set to 12 point. (You can always change the font size for a particular document if you wish; you'll learn how in "Changing Font, Font Size, and Font Style" later in this book.)

Customizing user information

4 Choose Tools, Options to display the Options dialog box. You can use this dialog box to set many preferences for Word's behavior.

5 Click the User Information tab, and enter your own information in the Name, Initials, and Mailing Address boxes. Click OK.

If you like, you can follow the general steps in this lesson to change the font and user information settings back to what they were once you've completed the lessons in this book.

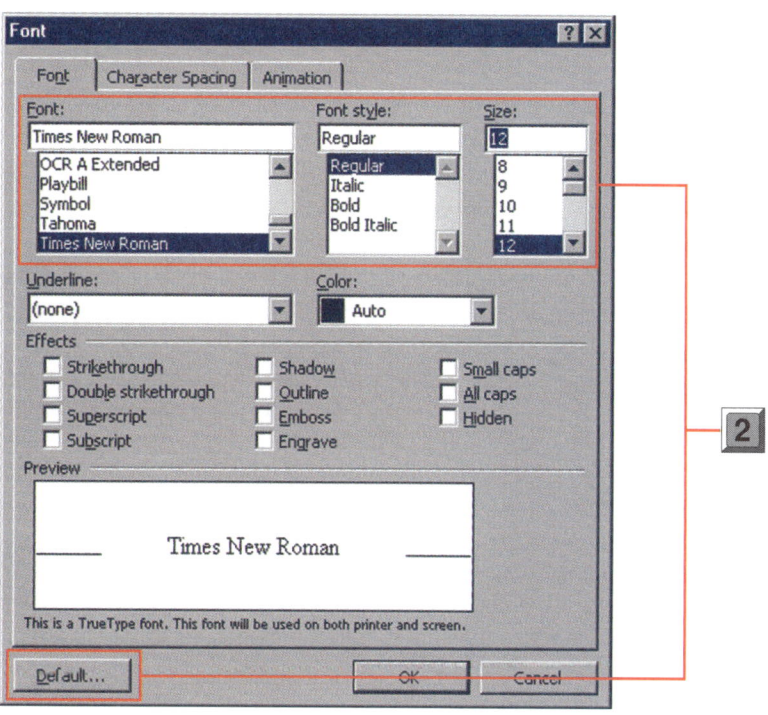

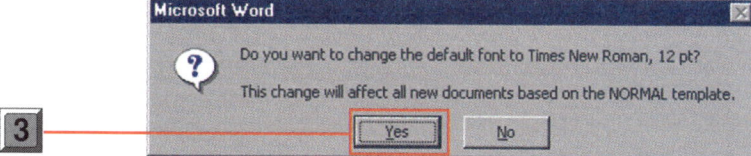

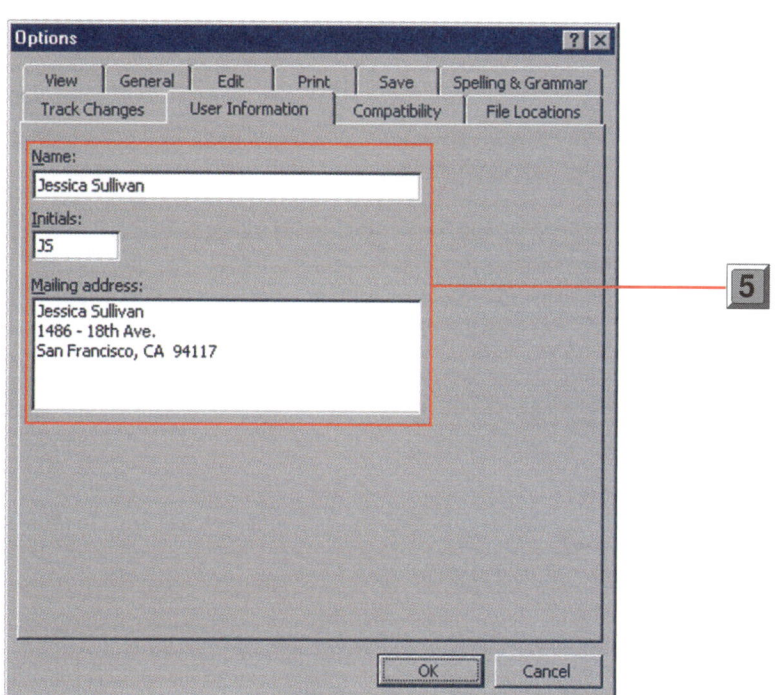

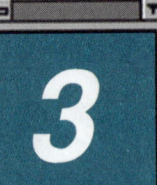

Getting Started

❖ **Switching Views and Zooming**

The first part of this lesson teaches you how to change the view of your document. Normal view, the default setting, is fine most of the time, but if you want to see text in the margin areas (such as headers and footers), you have to switch to Page Layout view. You also need to use Page Layout view to work with newspaper-style columns and graphics. Full Screen view clears everything off of your screen but your document, letting you see more of your text. The second part of this lesson explains how to change the magnification of your document on screen by adjusting the zoom setting.

Switching views

1 Start Word, and type **This lesson covers how to change views and zoom settings.** (It's easier to see how the views and zooming work if you have some text your document.) Then display the View menu, and choose Normal if it isn't already selected. The margin areas aren't visible in Normal view. And if your document is more than one page long, horizontal dotted lines indicate page breaks.

2 Choose View, Page Layout. Now the margin areas are visible, and page breaks are shown as actual separations between onscreen "pages" of text. Page Layout view also includes a vertical ruler on the left side of the document window.

3 Choose View, Full Screen. In Full Screen view, Word hides the title bar, menu bar, toolbars, and so on to give you a large, uncluttered view of your document. If you switch to Full Screen view from Page Layout view, the margin areas will be displayed. If you switch from Normal view, the margin areas will be hidden. To close Full Screen view, click the Close Full Screen button in the small Full Screen toolbar.

> ℹ️ You can also switch views by using the View buttons in the lower-left corner of the Word window. There are buttons for Normal view and Page Layout view, but not Full Screen view.

Zooming

4 Switch back to Page Layout view. Click the down arrow next to the Zoom box in the Standard toolbar, and choose 200%.

5 Your document is now displayed at 200% magnification. Increasing the magnification is helpful when you're working with small font sizes.

6 Display the Zoom list again, and this time choose Page Width.

7 Word decreases the magnification enough to show you the full width of the page in the window. Close Word without saving the document.

> ℹ️ The Whole Page and Two Pages options in the Zoom list are only available if you're using Page Layout view.

Getting Started

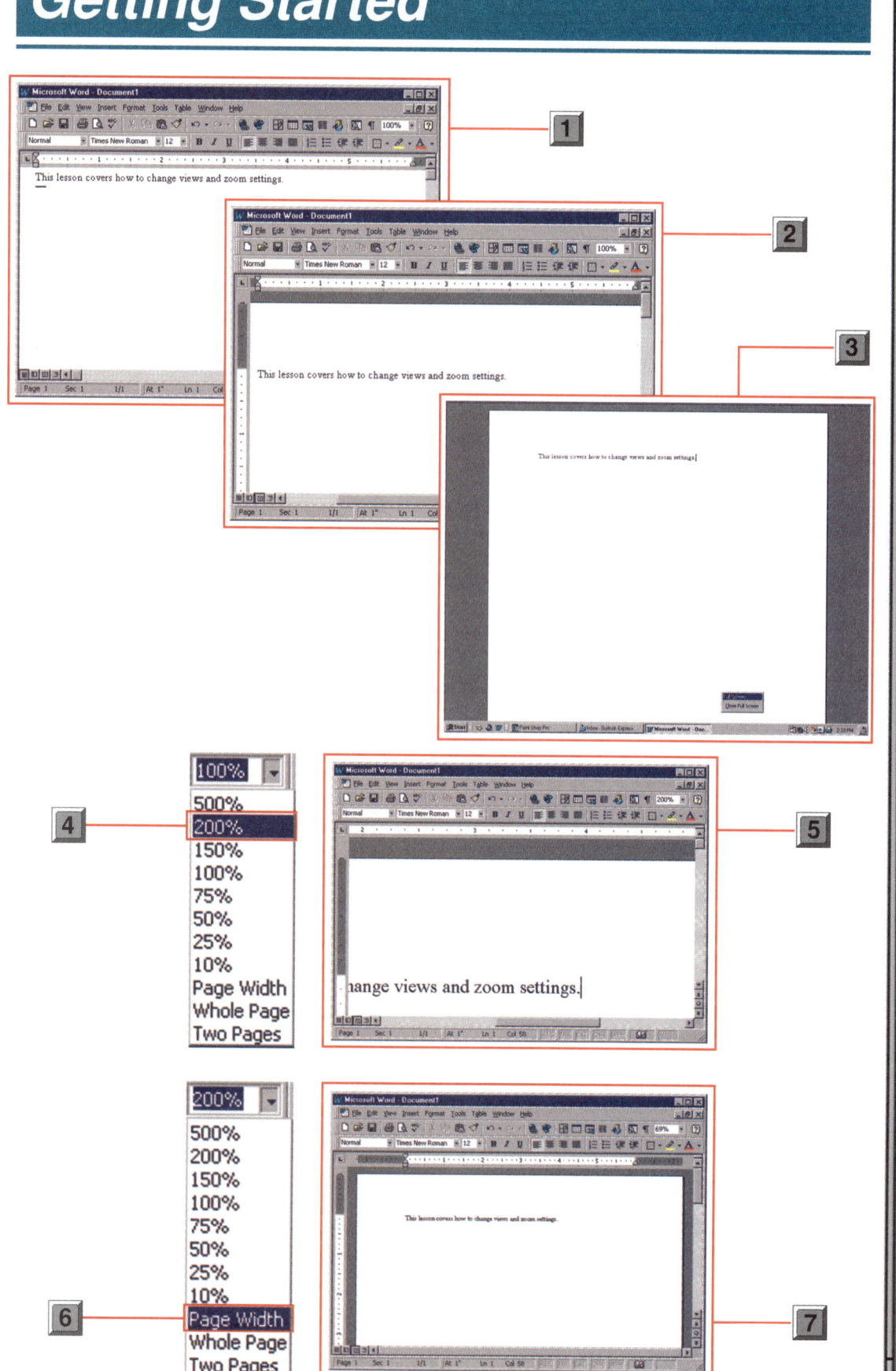

Normal
view

Page
Layout
view

Getting Started

4

❖ **Getting Help with the Office Assistant**

The Office Assistant offers tips on how to use Word more efficiently, assists with many tasks, alerts you to events that need your attention, and helps you search Word's help system. And it does all of this with animation and amusing sound effects (if your computer has a sound card).

1 Start Word. If the Office Assistant isn't currently displayed, click the Office Assistant button at the right end of the Standard toolbar.

2 The Office Assistant watches the tasks you perform, and when it has a tip about how to do something more efficiently, it displays a light bulb in the Office Assistant window. Click the light bulb to display the tip. (If the Office Assistant is not currently displayed, you can tell a tip is waiting because the Office Assistant toolbar button displays a light bulb. Click the Office Assistant button to view the Office Assistant and the tip.)

> **ⓘ** The default Office Assistant is a paper clip figure named *Clippit*. If you want to use one of the other eight assistants, right-click the Office Assistant window and click Choose Assistant in the context menu. The Office Assistant dialog box appears with the Gallery tab in front. Use the Next and Back buttons to check out the other assistants. When you find one you want to try, click OK. (You may need to insert your Office 97 CD to let Word copy the necessary files.)

3 After you've read the tip, click the Close button to close it.

> **ⓘ** Conveniently, the Office Assistant works the same in other Office applications such as Excel and PowerPoint. If you find the Office Assistant a bit annoying, however, you can haul it out of the way by dragging its title bar, or remove it from view entirely by clicking the Close box (the X) in its upper-right corner.

4 If you want the Office Assistant to search the online help system for a particular topic, click anywhere in the Office Assistant window (or press F1) to display a yellow box, type your search text, and click the Search button. For this example, type **envelopes** and click Search.

5 The Office Assistant finds several topics related to envelopes. Click the blue button next to Print an Address on an Envelope.

6 The Office Assistant displays the information from Word's help system. Click the Close box in the upper-right corner of the help window to close it. Then click the Close box in the upper-right corner of the Word window to close the application.

> **ⓘ** If you prefer a more businesslike approach to getting help, try out Word's Help Topics dialog box (choose Help, Contents and Index). The Contents tab lets you investigate a variety of general topics (book icons that you double-click to display related topics), and specific topics (question-mark icons that you double-click to display help screens of information). The Index tab lets you type in the topic you want to find out more about. In many cases, the Office Assistant and the Help Topics dialog box ultimately lead you to the same information; which one you use boils down to personal preference.

Getting Started

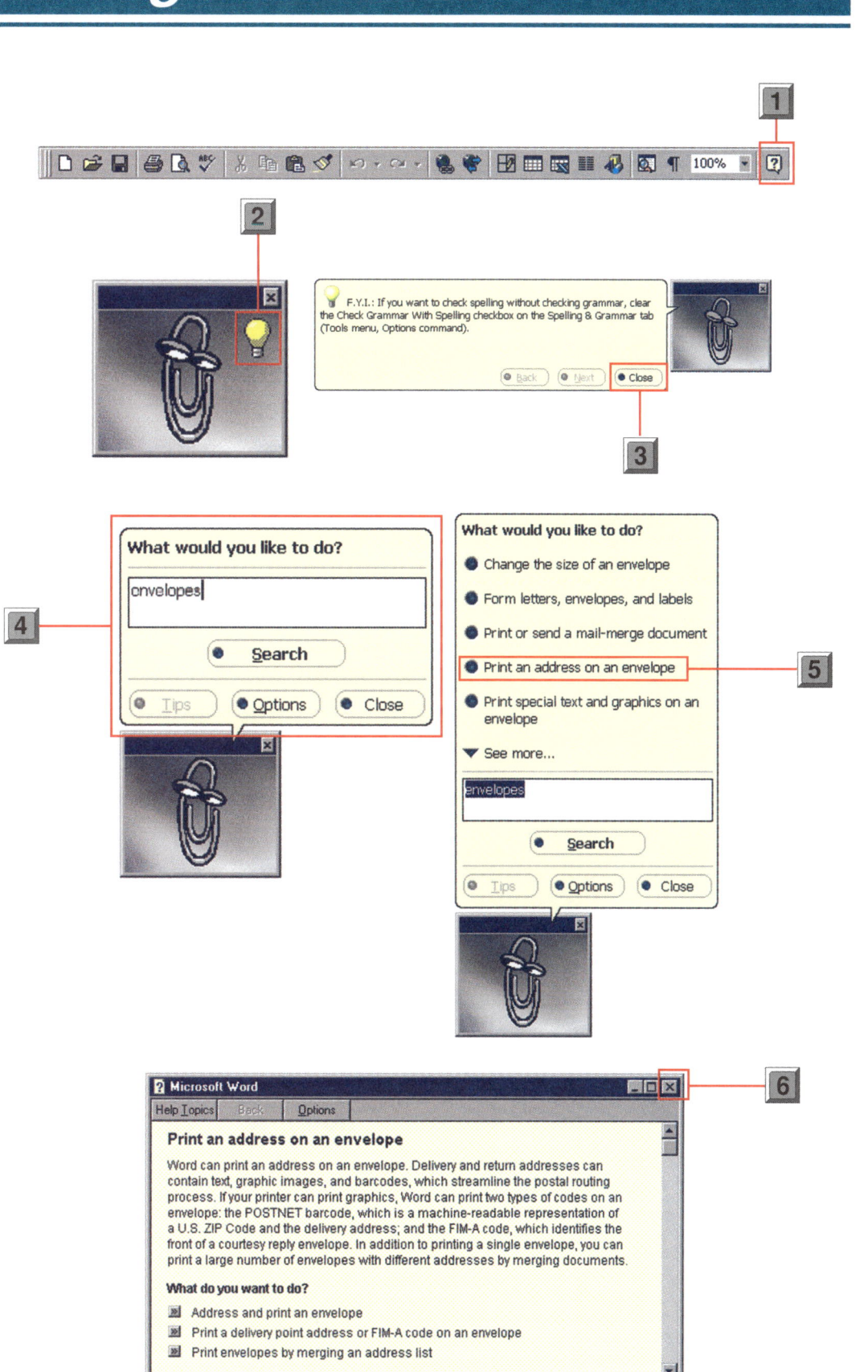

1

2

F.Y.I.: If you want to check spelling without checking grammar, clear the Check Grammar With Spelling checkbox on the Spelling & Grammar tab (Tools menu, Options command).

Back   Next   ● Close

3

What would you like to do?

envelopes

● Search

○ Tips   ● Options   ● Close

4

What would you like to do?

● Change the size of an envelope

● Form letters, envelopes, and labels

● Print or send a mail-merge document

● Print an address on an envelope

● Print special text and graphics on an envelope

▼ See more...

envelopes

● Search

○ Tips   ● Options   ● Close

5

Microsoft Word   _ □ ×

Help Topics   Back   Options

Print an address on an envelope

Word can print an address on an envelope. Delivery and return addresses can contain text, graphic images, and barcodes, which streamline the postal routing process. If your printer can print graphics, Word can print two types of codes on an envelope: the POSTNET barcode, which is a machine-readable representation of a U.S. ZIP Code and the delivery address; and the FIM-A code, which identifies the front of a courtesy reply envelope. In addition to printing a single envelope, you can print a large number of envelopes with different addresses by merging documents.

What do you want to do?

▣ Address and print an envelope

▣ Print a delivery point address or FIM-A code on an envelope

▣ Print envelopes by merging an address list

6

Office
Assistant

Working with Documents

5

❖ **Typing a Letter**

In this lesson, you type a brief business letter. In the next lesson, you will save the letter, which you will use to learn other Word 97 skills later in this book.

1 Start Word. Word opens with a new blank document.

Starting a new document

2 If you already have Word open and you're working on another document, you can click the New button in the Standard toolbar (or press Ctrl+N) to start a new blank document.

3 Type the text below. Press Enter to end short lines of text, to end paragraphs, and to create blank lines. For lines of text within a paragraph, don't press Enter at the end of the line. Word will wrap the text to the next line for you.

October 2, 1998

Mr. John Sanders
Sanders Corporation
123 Main Street
Seattle, WA 98101

Dear Mr. Sanders:

Thank you for your interest in Superior Widgets.

As you will recall from our discussion yesterday, Superior Widgets are designed and guaranteed to last ten years without maintenance of any kind.

I will be calling you next week to see if you have any questions about the enclosed brochure.

Sincerely,

Melissa Johnson

---

4 Go on to the next lesson without closing Word.

ℹ️ The New toolbar button assumes you want to base your new document on the *Normal template*. All documents are based on a template, which is like a blueprint for a document. The Normal template contains the formatting for a standard blank document. Other templates that come with Word contain both formatting and text to help you create specialized types of documents, such as fax cover sheets, memos, and so on. You'll learn how to use other templates in "Creating a Fax Cover Sheet Using a Template" later in this book.

Working with Documents

Press Ctrl+N to start a new document

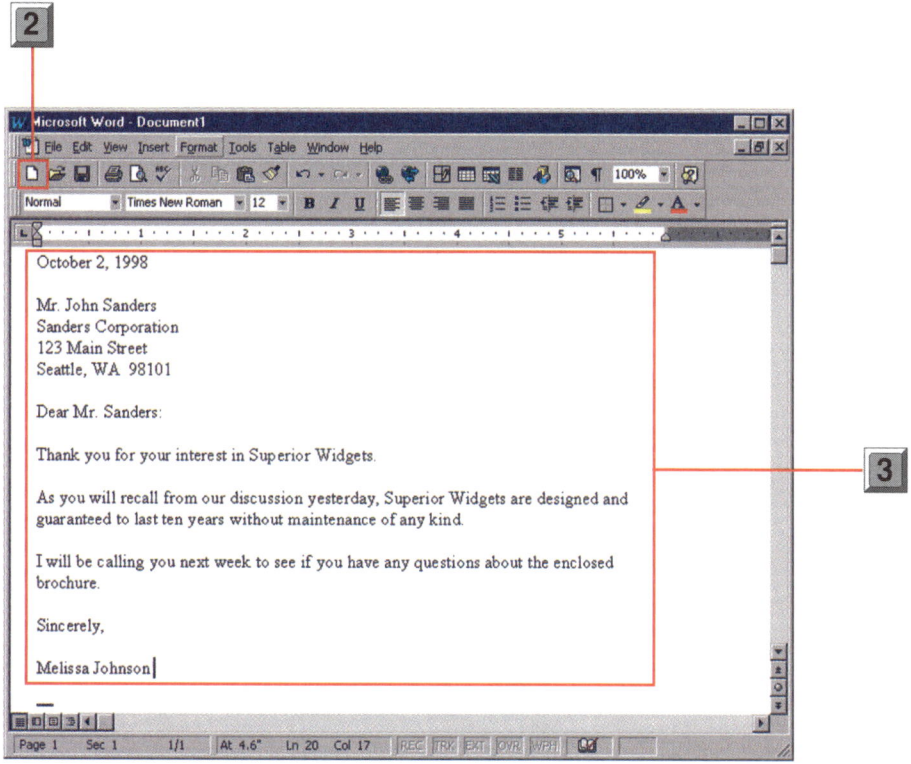

New

11

Working with Documents

6

❖ Saving a Document

In this lesson, you learn how to save the document you created in the previous lesson. The letter you typed should still be open on your screen.

1 Click the Save button in the Standard toolbar. (You can also choose File, Save or press Ctrl+S.)

> ℹ Because this is the first time you've saved this document, Word presents you with the Save As dialog box. You use this dialog box to give the document a name and tell Word what folder to store it in.

2 Display the Save In drop-down list at the top of the Save As dialog box, and choose C: (your local hard drive).

3 Double-click the My Documents folder. (Microsoft Office automatically creates this folder during installation. If you don't have a My Documents folder, you can pick another folder to save this practice document in.)

4 Click the Up One Level button. This button quickly takes you back to the contents of the C: drive. You can use this button whenever you want to move up one level in the folder structure on your computer (or network). Now double-click the My Documents folder again to redisplay the contents of that folder. (The My Documents folder should appear in the Save In box.)

5 Note the name October 2 in the File Name box. Word by default uses the first few words in the document as the file name. Using the mouse, drag over the name to select (highlight) it. Then type over it with the name **Reply to Sanders**, and click the Save button.

6 The name Reply to Sanders now appears in the title bar of the document window. Press Ctrl+End to move to the end of the letter, press Enter if necessary to move to the line directly beneath Melissa Johnson, and type **Sales Representative**.

7 Click the Save button in the Standard toolbar again (or choose File, Save). This time Word does not display the Save As dialog box. Because you have already named your document, Word assumes that you want to keep the same name. It immediately saves the document, overwriting the original letter with the revised one.

> ℹ If you want to save a revised document with a different name so that Word doesn't overwrite the original, choose File, Save As instead of File, Save. Then you can specify a new name and/or location for the revised document in the Save As dialog box.

8 Close the Reply to Sanders document and then close Word.

Working with Documents

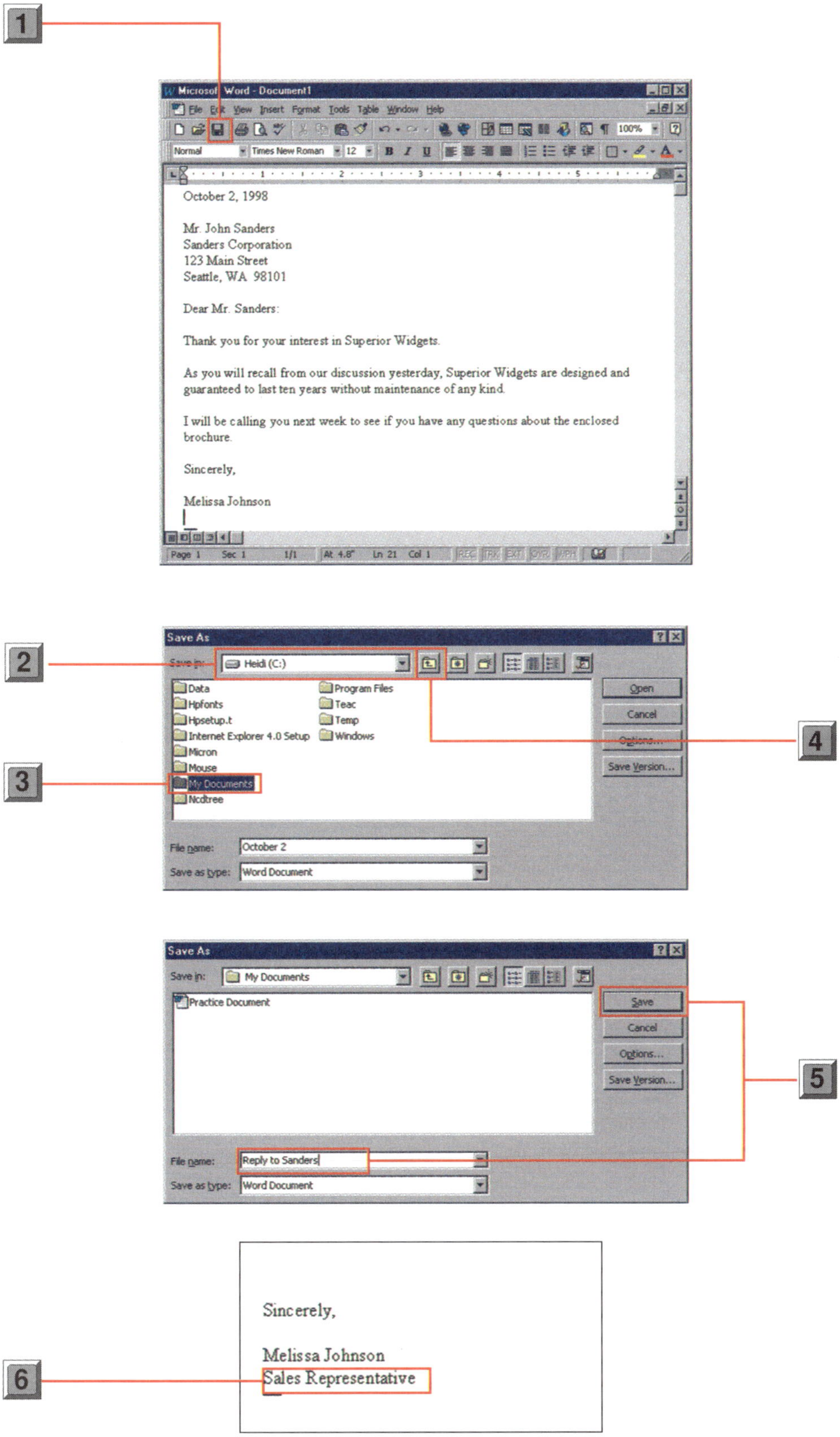

6

Quick Reference Bar

Press Ctrl+S to save a document

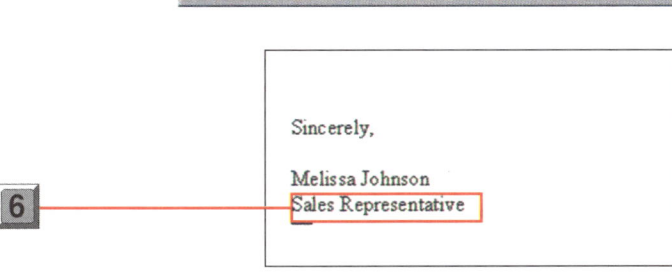

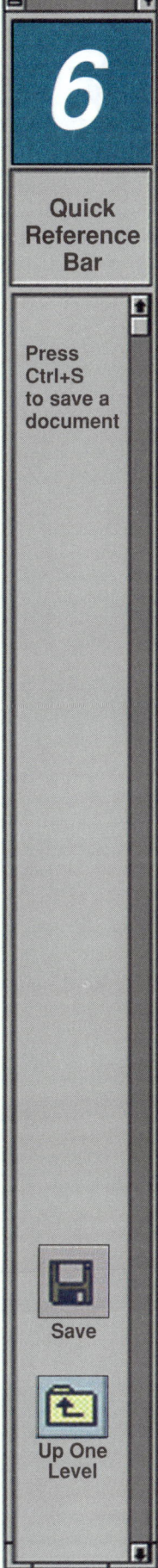

Save

Up One Level

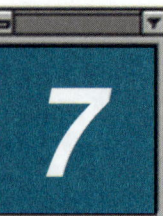

Working with Documents

❖ Opening and Navigating in a Document

In this lesson, you open the letter you saved in the previous lesson, and then you learn different ways of moving the insertion point (the cursor) in a document.

Opening a document

1 Click the Open button in the Standard toolbar. (You can also choose File, Open or press Ctrl+O.)

2 Word displays the Open dialog box. Note that it looks very much like the Save As dialog box. Drop down the Look In list at the top of the dialog box and choose C: (your local hard drive). Then double-click the My Documents folder, click the Reply to Sanders document, and click the Open button.

> ℹ️ Word lists the four files you've worked with most recently at the bottom of the File menu. To open one of these four files, simply display the File menu and click the desired file name.

Navigating with the keyboard

3 Press the Down Arrow key repeatedly to move the insertion point to the beginning of the line *As you will recall*…Press Ctrl+Right Arrow to move the insertion point word by word to the beginning of the word *yesterday*. Press Ctrl+Delete to delete the word, add a space, and then type *last week*.

4 Press the Down Arrow key three times to move to the line beginning with *I will be calling you*, and press the End key to move to the end of the line, after the word *enclosed*. Type *product* followed by a space.

5 Press Ctrl+End to move to the end of the document. Press Enter to create a new line under *Sales Representative*, and type *Western Division*. Then press Ctrl+Home to move to the beginning of the document.

Navigating with the mouse

6 Position the mouse pointer (the I-beam) just before the word next in the last paragraph of the letter and click once to move the insertion point to the new location. Type *on Monday or Tuesday* and add a space.

7 Click the Up and Down scroll arrows at the top and bottom of the vertical scroll bar a few times. Clicking the scroll arrows scrolls the document one line at a time.

> ℹ️ Using the vertical scroll bar does not move the insertion point. The insertion point doesn't move until you click where you want to edit the text.

8 Drag the scroll box to the bottom of the scroll bar and then back up to the top. This is a fast way of bringing the end and the beginning of a long document into view.

9 Save and Close the Reply to Sanders document, and then close Word.

Working with Documents

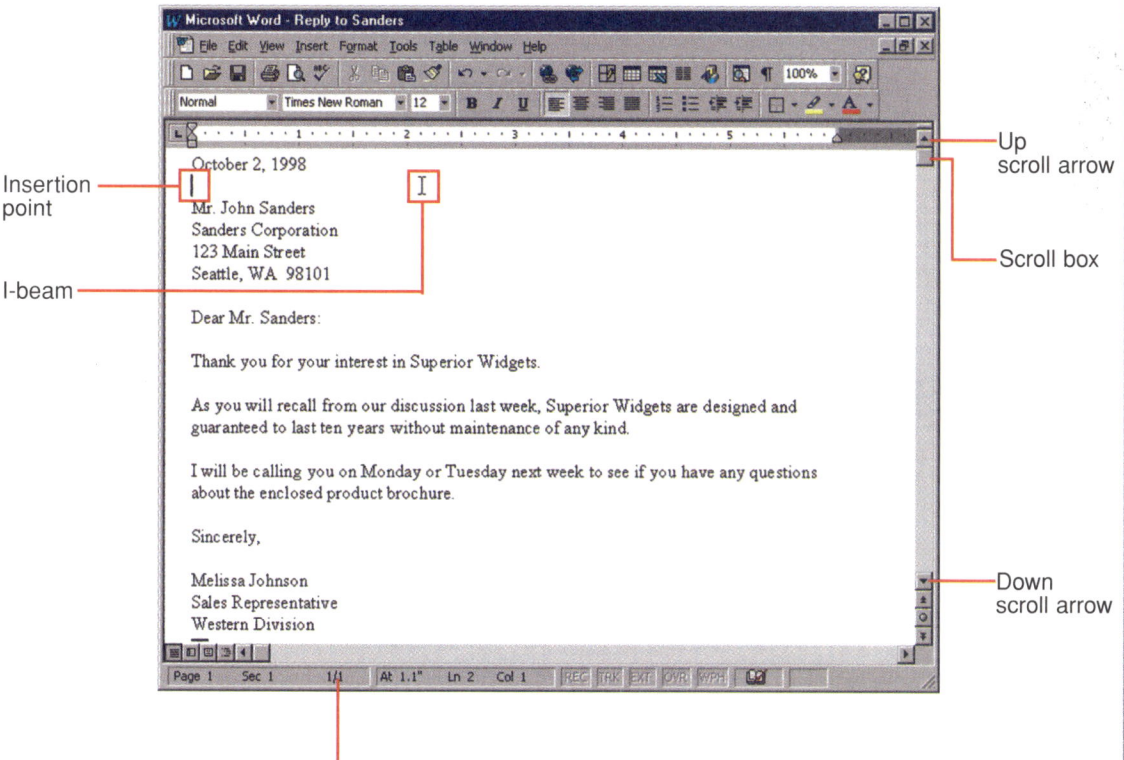

Insertion point

I-beam

Up scroll arrow

Scroll box

Down scroll arrow

Current and total number of pages

Navigating with the Keyboard

One character to right	**Right Arrow key**
One character to left	**Left Arrow key**
One line up	**Up Arrow key**
One line down	**Down Arrow key**
One word to right	**Ctrl+Right Arrow**
One word to left	**Ctrl+Left Arrow**
One paragraph up	**Ctrl+Up Arrow**
One paragraph down	**Ctrl+Down Arrow**
End of line	**End**
Beginning of line	**Home**
Bottom of screen	**Page Down**
Top of screen	**Page Up**
End of document	**Ctrl+End**
Beginning of document	**Ctrl+Home**
Previous editing location	**Shift+F5**

Working with Documents

❖ Selecting Text

In this lesson you open the Reply to Sanders letter you revised in the previous lesson, and use it to learn how to select (highlight) text. You have to select text before you can format it, cut and paste it, and perform many other actions as well.

1 Open the Reply to Sanders letter from the My Documents folder. First you will merge the second and third paragraphs into one paragraph. To do this, click directly after the end of the first paragraph (after *any kind.*). Press the Delete key two times to delete the hard returns separating the paragraphs, and then add a space.

2 Position the I-beam directly in front of the word *from* in the second paragraph of the letter, and drag through the word *week.* Then click once to deselect the text. (If you don't click to deselect, the text will automatically be deselected as soon as you select something else.)

> ℹ️ Dragging lets you select any amount of text, but if you need to select a word, sentence, paragraph or the entire document, the shortcuts described in the remaining steps are faster and more accurate.

3 Point to the word *interest* in the first paragraph and double-click to select it.

4 Position the I-beam anywhere over the sentence beginning *I will be calling you on*, and hold down the Ctrl key as you click once to select the sentence.

5 Position the mouse pointer to the left of the line *Seattle, WA 98101.* When it becomes a white arrow angled to the right (pointing to the line of text), click to select it.

6 Position the mouse pointer to the left of the middle paragraph. When it becomes a white arrow angled toward the paragraph, double-click to select the paragraph.

7 Keep the mouse pointer on the far left edge of the document window (the mouse pointer should still be a white arrow), and triple-click. The whole document is now selected. (You can press Ctrl+A to accomplish the same thing.)

> ℹ️ You can select text with the keyboard by clicking just in front of the text and then pressing Shift+Right Arrow to select the text one character at a time. You can also press Shift+Left Arrow to select character by character to the left, or Shift+Up Arrow or Shift+Down Arrow to select a line at a time.

8 Close the document without saving it and then close Word.

Working with Documents

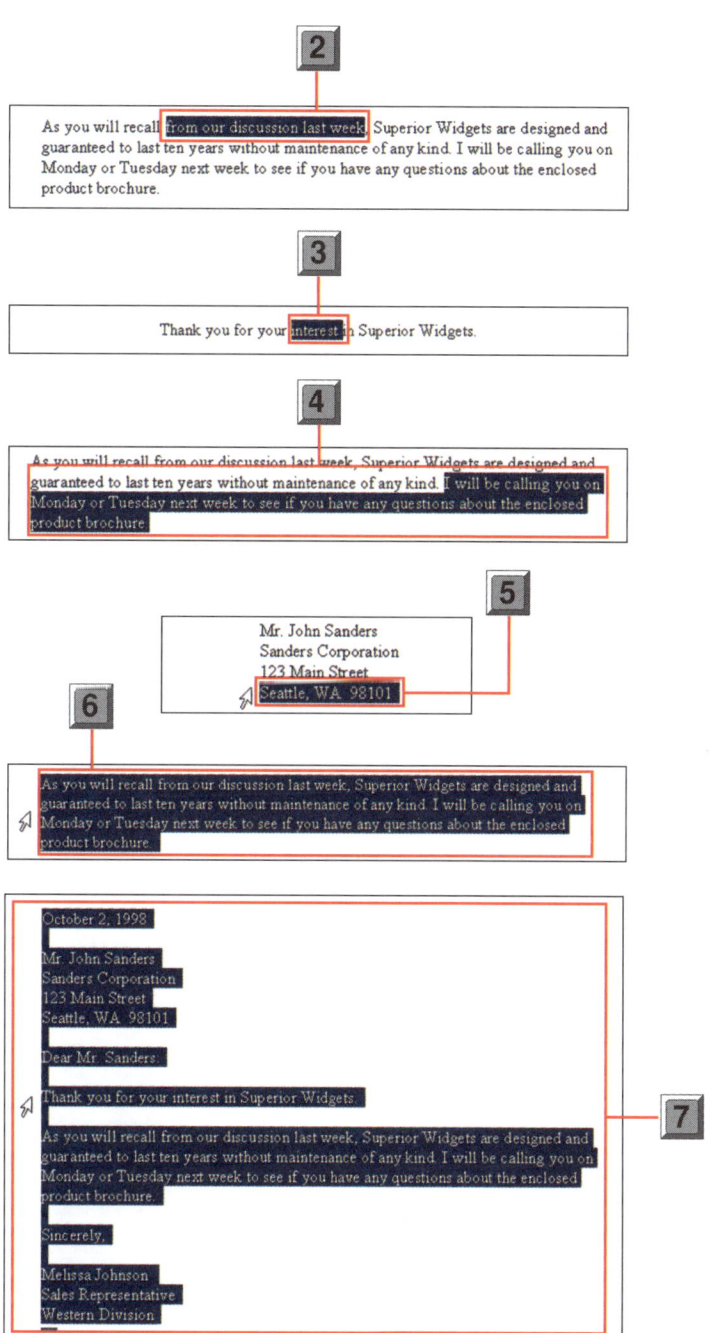

Press
Ctrl+A
to select
the entire
document

Selecting Text

Any amount of text	**Drag across the text**
One word	**Double-click on the word**
One sentence	**Ctrl+click on the sentence**
One line	**Click to the left of the line**
One paragraph	**Double-click to the left of the paragraph**
Entire document	**Triple-click to the left of the document**

Working with Documents

9

❖ **Using Undo and Redo**

In this lesson, you learn how to use the Undo command, an indispensable tool that lets you reverse recent actions such as typing text, deleting text, cutting and pasting, and formatting. If you undo something and change your mind, you can use the Redo command to reverse the undo. To learn about Undo and Redo, you will select, delete, and format text. You'll learn more about all of these skills later in this book.

1 Start Word, and open the Reply to Sanders letter from your My Documents folder.

2 Double-click the word *Corporation* in the address block to select it.

3 Type over the selected word with **Company**.

4 Point to the Undo button in the Standard toolbar. You'll see a ToolTip showing your most recent action, typing. Click the button (or press Ctrl+Z) to reverse the action. Then click once to deselect the text.

5 Click the Redo button (or press Ctrl+Y) to redo the action you just undid.

> ℹ️ You can click the Undo button or the Redo button multiple times to undo or redo previous actions one by one. If, when you point to the Undo or Redo button, the ToolTip states *Can't Undo* or *Can't Redo*, there aren't any actions that you can undo or redo.

6 Now you'll perform three actions to practice undoing all three of them at once. First, position your mouse pointer at the beginning of the paragraph beginning with *As you will recall*, drag through to the end of the paragraph to select it, and press the Delete key to delete it. Next, drag across the name *Melissa Johnson* at the end of the letter, and click the Bold button in the Formatting toolbar (it shows a B) to apply boldface. Finally, click after the word *Representative* in the signature block, add a space, and then type **and Telemarketing Associate**.

7 Display the Undo drop-down list. The actions you have performed in this lesson appear in the list, with the most recent one at the top. Click Clear to reverse all three actions you performed in step 6.

8 Close the document without saving it, and then close Word.

Working with Documents

Quick
Reference
Bar

Press
Ctrl+Z
to undo

Press
Ctrl+Y
to redo

2

3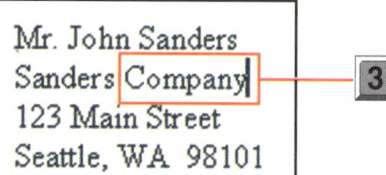

4

5

October 2, 1998

Mr. John Sanders
Sanders Company
123 Main Street
Seattle, WA 98101

Dear Mr. Sanders:

Thank you for your interest in Superior Widgets.

Sincerely,

Melissa Johnson
Sales Representative and Telemarketing Associate
Western Division

6

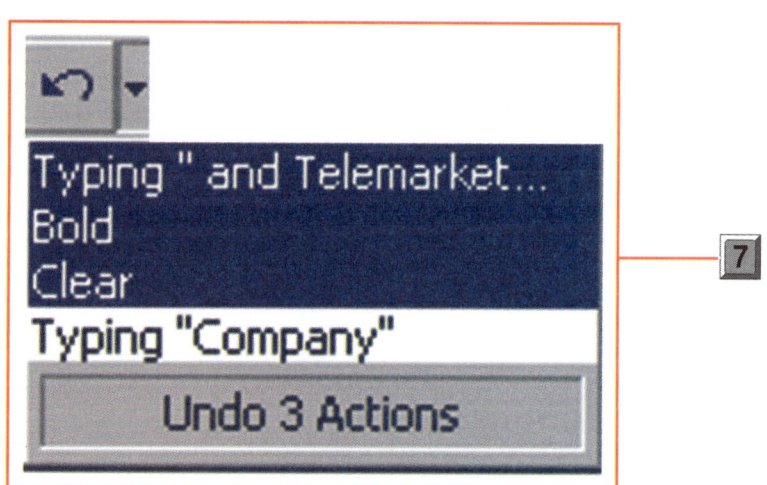

7

Formatting

10

❖ **Changing Font, Font Size, and Font Style**

You can format the text in your document by changing its font, the font size (measured in points—the larger the number, the bigger the font), and the font style (bold, italic, and underline). When you apply character formatting, it works best to select the text before issuing the formatting command.

Using the Formatting toolbar

1 Start Word, and open the Reply to Sanders letter from the My Documents folder. Then triple-click to the left of the text or press Ctrl+A to select the entire letter.

2 Display the Font drop-down list in the Formatting toolbar, and choose Arial.

> **ℹ** Word lists the fonts you use the most frequently above the double-line in the Font list. Below the double-line is an alphabetical list of all the fonts installed on your computer.

3 Display the Font Size list, and choose 11. Then click once to deselect the text.

4 Drag across *Superior Widgets* in the first paragraph of the letter and click the Bold button in the Formatting toolbar (or press Ctrl+B). Click to deselect the text. Then boldface *Superior Widgets* in the second paragraph as well.

5 Select *ten years* in the second paragraph and click the Italic button in the Formatting toolbar (or press Ctrl+I). Keeping the text selected, click the Underline button in the Formatting toolbar (or press Ctrl+U).

> **ℹ** To remove boldface, italics, or underlining from a block of text, select the text, and then click the Bold, Italic, or Underline button again. If you want to remove all character formatting from a block of text, select it and then press Ctrl+Spacebar.

Using the Font dialog box

6 If you want to preview your formatting changes before you apply them to the text, you can use the Font dialog box instead of the Formatting toolbar. Select the entire document, and then choose Format, Font and click the Font tab if it isn't already in front. Scroll through the Font list and click on a few different fonts. The Preview area at the bottom of the dialog box shows you what the selected font looks like. When you find one you want to use, click it, and then click OK.

7 Close the document and Word without saving the changes.

Formatting

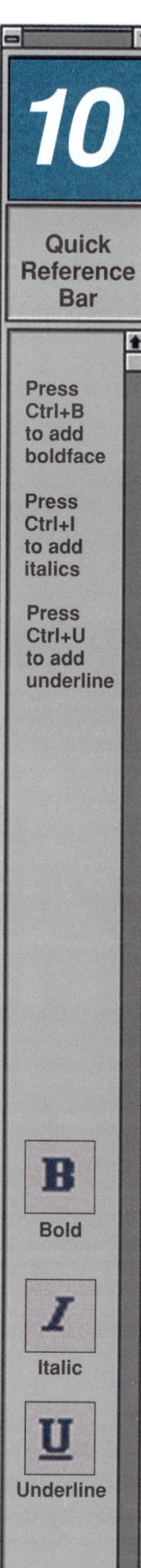

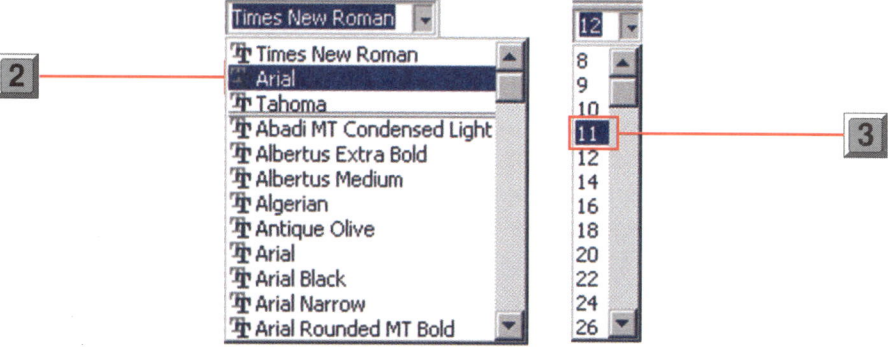

2

3

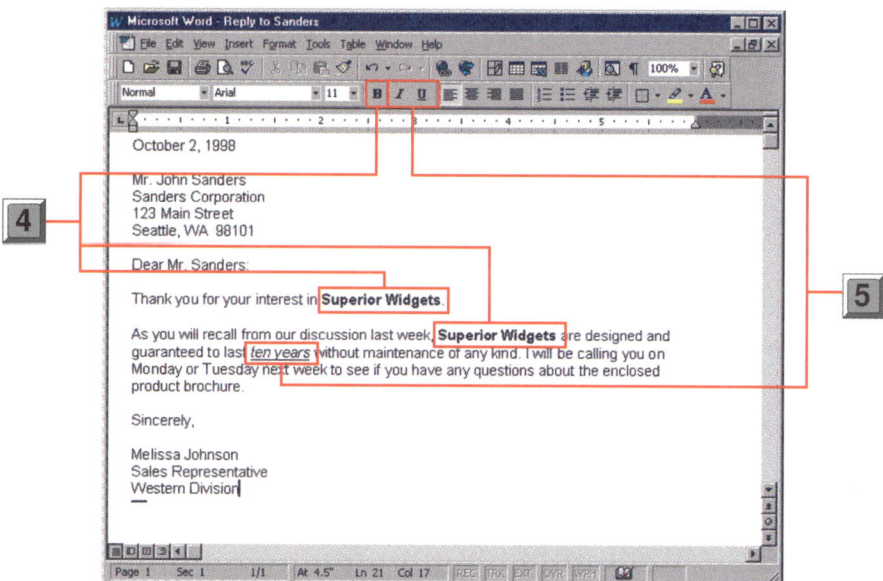

4

5

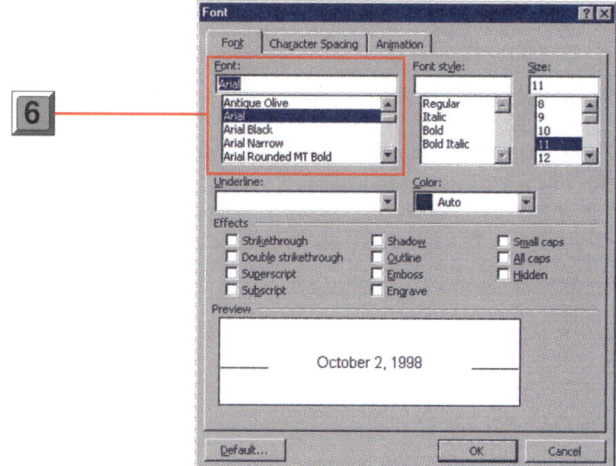

6

Quick Reference Bar

Press Ctrl+B to add boldface

Press Ctrl+I to add italics

Press Ctrl+U to add underline

B

Bold

I

Italic

U

Underline

Formatting

11

❖ **Changing Alignment, Indentation, and Line Spacing**

Word automatically formats your document with left alignment, no indention, and single line spacing. This lesson shows you how to change these default settings. The three formatting features discussed in this lesson are all paragraph formatting, meaning that they affect your text paragraph by paragraph. (Word considers a paragraph to be any block of text, even a short line, that you end by pressing Enter.) If no text is selected when you issue one of these commands, you will change only the paragraph that contains the insertion point. If you want to change several paragraphs (or all of the paragraphs in the document) make sure to select them all first.

Changing alignment

1 Start Word and open the Reply to Sanders letter.

2 Click anywhere in the paragraph *October 2, 1998*. Then click the Align Right button in the Formatting toolbar.

3 Click just after the Zip code in the address block, press Enter twice, and then type **Re: Superior Widgets product information**. With the insertion point still on this line of text, click the Center button in the Formatting toolbar. Then select the line, and click the Bold button.

> ℹ️ In addition to right and center alignment, you can justify a paragraph. Justification produces a straight right and left edge. If you want to experiment with justified alignment, click in the paragraph beginning with *As you will recall*, and click the Justify button in the Formatting toolbar.

Changing indentation

4 Select the four paragraphs in the closing of the letter (from *Sincerely* to *Western Division*), and drag the Left Indent marker (the square) out to the 3.75" mark on the ruler. Click to deselect the text, and then save the letter.

> ℹ️ If you want to create a hanging indent (with the first line of the paragraph extending out to the left of the remaining lines), drag the Hanging Indent marker (the lower triangle). If you only want to indent the first line of a paragraph, drag the First Line Indent marker (the upper triangle).

Changing line spacing

5 Press Ctrl+A or triple-click to the left of the text to select the entire document, and choose Format, Paragraph to display the Paragraph dialog box.

6 Click the Indents and Spacing tab if it isn't already in front, display the Line Spacing drop-down list, and choose 1.5 lines. Then click OK.

7 Close Word without saving the changes you made after step 4.

Formatting

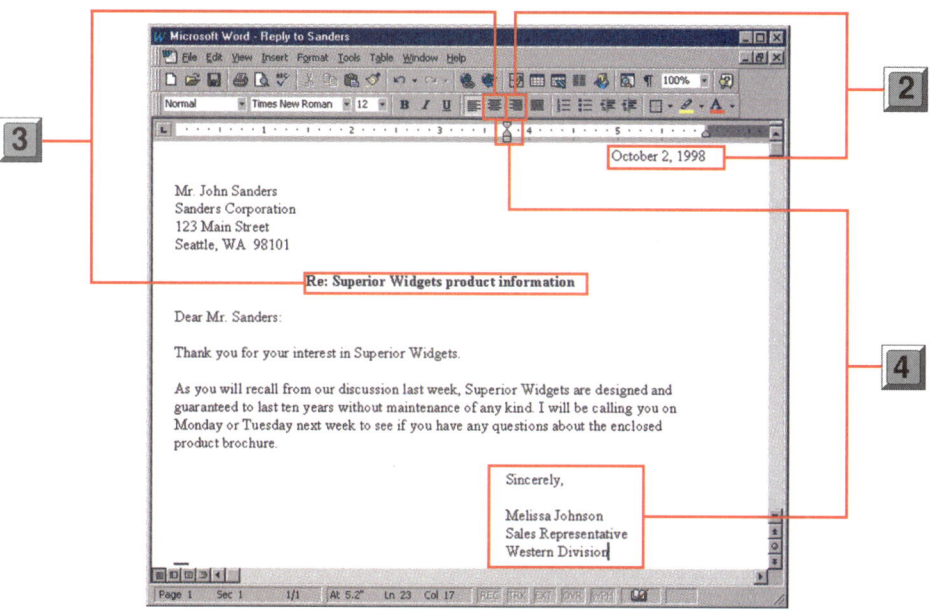

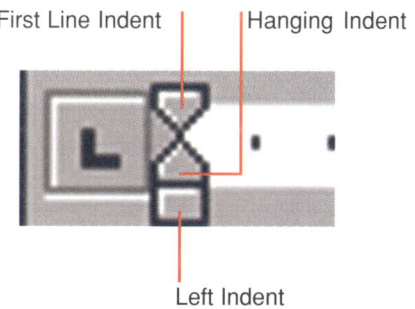

First Line Indent   Hanging Indent

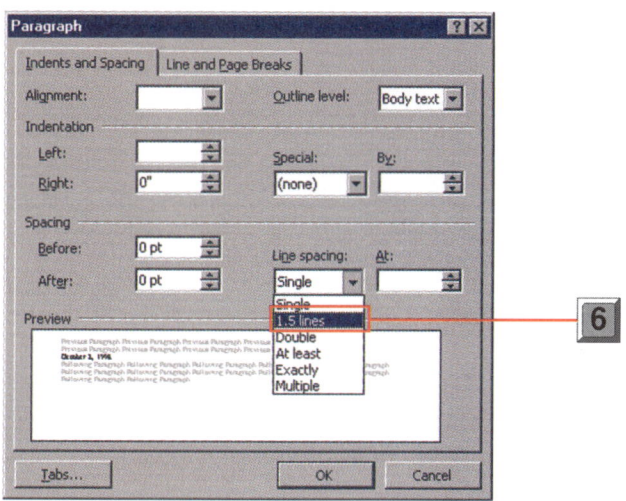

Left Indent

Quick Reference Bar

Press
Ctrl+L
to left align

Press
Ctrl+E
to center

Press
Ctrl+R
to right align

Press
Ctrl+J
to justify

Press
Ctrl+M
to indent
.5 inches

Press
Shift+Ctrl+M
to unindent
.5 inches

Press Ctrl+2
to double
space,
Ctrl+5 to 1.5
line space,
and Ctrl+1 to
single space

Align Left

Center

Align Right

Justify

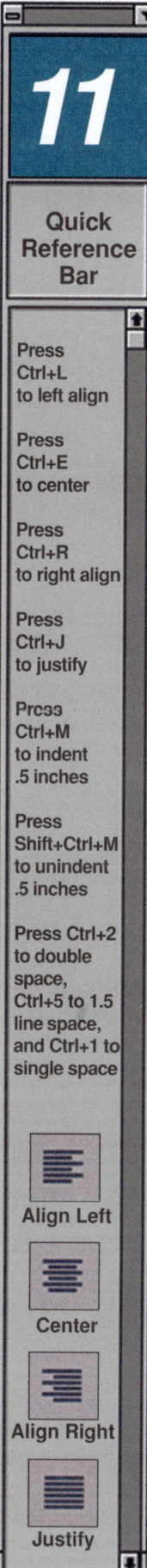

Formatting

❖ Setting Custom Tabs

Word's default tabs are positioned every half inch across the ruler (they show up as faint gray tick marks). Each time you press the Tab key, your insertion point moves to the next tab stop, pushing over any text to right of the insertion point. In regular body text, these default tabs work just fine. When you want to create a list with two or more columns of text, however, it's easier if you replace the default tabs with custom tabs positioned exactly where you want to line up your text.

1 Start Word and open the Reply to Sanders letter from the My Documents folder. Click just after *brochure.* at the end of the paragraph above the signature block, and press Enter two times. Then type **In the meantime, here is a price list for our key products:** and press Enter two more times.

2 Click in the ruler at the 1.25" mark to add a left tab. The default tab stops to the left of the custom tab automatically disappear.

> Word assumes you want to create a left tab, which left-aligns text at the tab stop. However, you can also create three other types of tabs: center, right, and decimal. Center tabs center text at the tab stop, right tabs right-align text at the tab stop, and decimal tabs align numbers at the decimal point. You specify which type of tab you want to insert by clicking one or more times on the Tab Alignment button at the left end of the ruler.

3 Click the Tab Alignment button three times so that the decimal tab is showing. Then click in the ruler at the 4.25" mark to insert a decimal tab.

4 Press the Tab key once to move the insertion point to the first custom tab and type **Yellow Mini Widget**. Press Tab again to move to the second custom tab and type **$19.99**. Press Enter to move to the next line. Add the two lines shown below to the list, pressing Tab before each entry and Enter at the end of each line. Then press Enter once more to add a blank line above the signature block.

       Green Standard Widget $59.99
       Blue Jumbo Widget $109.99

5 Select all three lines (paragraphs) in the list, point to the left tab, drag it along the ruler to the 1.5" mark, and release the mouse button. (Make sure you're pointing directly at the tab stop or you'll unintentionally insert a new custom tab.) Then drag the left tab back to the 1.25" mark. (You have to select all of the paragraphs in a list before dragging a tab, otherwise Word only moves the tab in the paragraph containing the insertion point.)

6 Save the document, and then close Word.

> To delete a custom tab, point to it on the ruler, drag down into the text area, and then release the mouse button. As soon as you delete a custom tab, the default tabs to the left of the custom tab automatically reappear. To see what custom tabs are in effect for a certain paragraph, click anywhere in the paragraph, and then look at the ruler.

Formatting

Tab Alignment
button

Default tab stops

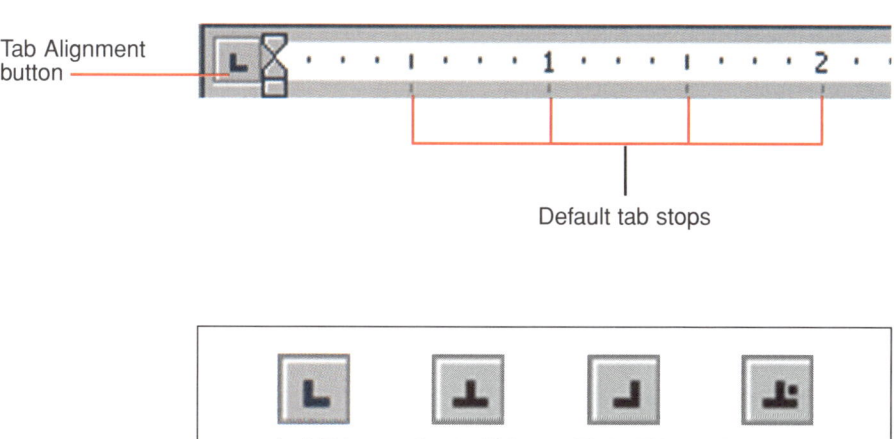

| Left Tab | Center Tab | Right Tab | Decimal Tab |

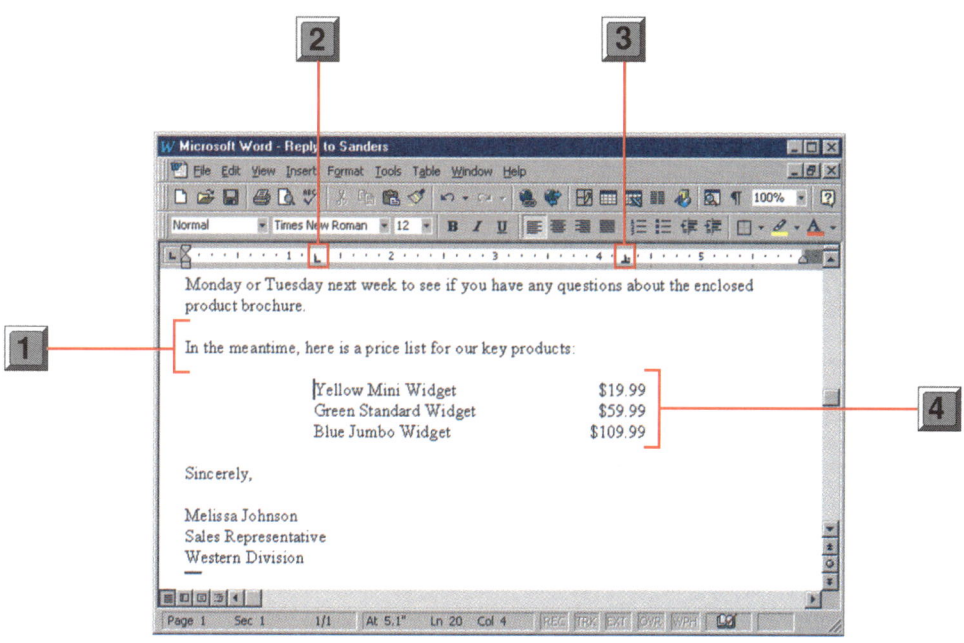

Monday or Tuesday next week to see if you have any questions about the enclosed product brochure.

In the meantime, here is a price list for our key products:

Yellow Mini Widget $19.99
Green Standard Widget $59.99
Blue Jumbo Widget $109.99

Sincerely,

Melissa Johnson
Sales Representative
Western Division

Formatting

❖ **Creating Numbered and Bulleted Lists**

Word makes it easy to create numbered and bulleted lists by adding the numbers or bullets for you, and by indenting the text so that it doesn't wrap underneath the numbers or bullets. What's more, when you type the first item in a list and press Enter, Word turns on the numbered or bulleted list feature automatically.

1 Start Word, or, if Word is already open, click the New button in the Standard toolbar to start a new document.

2 Type the title of the list, **Notes for Housesitter**, and press Enter twice. Type **1.**, add a space, and then type **We will be gone until the evening of July 14. You can reach us at 415-865-4737.** and press Enter. Word turns on the numbered list feature and inserts a *2.* on the next line. Note that the Numbering button on the Formatting toolbar now looks like it's pushed in. (If the feature doesn't turn on, read the tip at the end of this lesson.)

> ℹ️ If you want to start a bulleted list instead of a numbered list, type an asterisk (*) followed by a space, type the text for the first item, and then press Enter. Word automatically turns on the bulleted list feature and converts the asterisk into a bullet.

3 Type the remaining lines shown in the figure on the facing page, pressing Enter after each item. Then press Enter a second time after the last item to turn off the numbered list feature.

4 Click just after the first item in the list (after *reach us at 415-865-4737.*) and press Shift+Enter to create blank line underneath the item. Do the same for the second and third items.

> ℹ️ Word inserts a number or bullet at the beginning of each paragraph, or item, in a numbered or bulleted list. Every time you press Enter you generate a new paragraph. Pressing Shift+Enter instead inserts a *line-break character*, which breaks the line without ending the paragraph, and prevents Word from adding a bullet or number to the new line.

5 Select all of the items in the list, and click the Bullets button in the Formatting toolbar to change the numbers to bullets.

6 Click anywhere to deselect the text, and save the document with the name **Vacation Notes** in the My Documents folder, and then close the document and close Word.

> ℹ️ If Word does not automatically turn on the numbered and bulleted list features, choose Tools, AutoCorrect, click the AutoFormat As You Type tab, mark the Automatic Bulleted Lists and Automatic Numbered Lists check boxes, and then click OK. If you find these automatic features annoying and want to turn them off, follow the same steps but clear the check boxes. If you turn them off, you can always turn them on "manually" when you want to create a list by placing the insertion point on the line where you want to start the list, and clicking the Numbering or Bullets button in the Formatting toolbar.

Formatting

Numbering

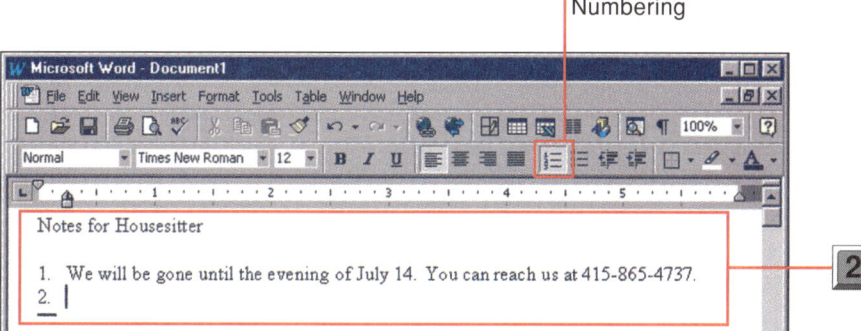

Bullets

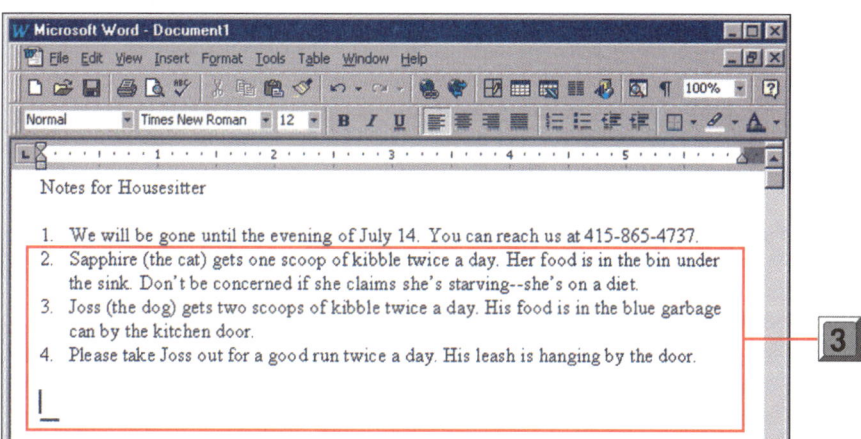

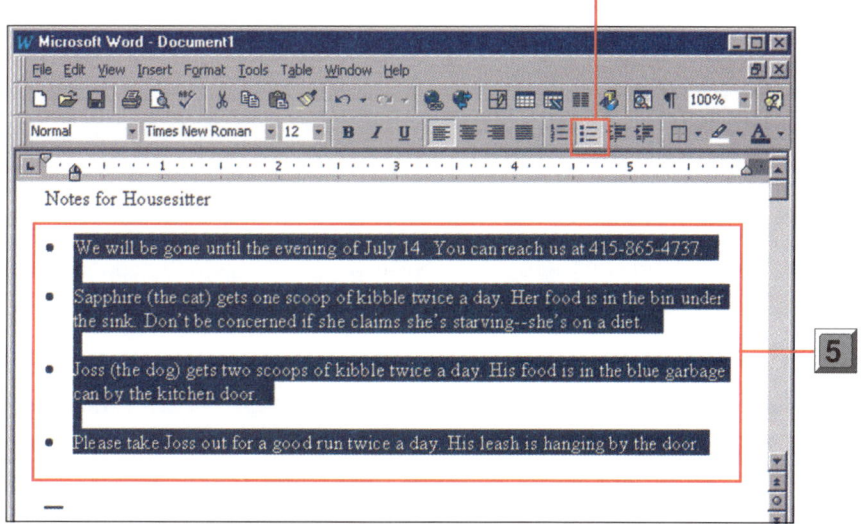

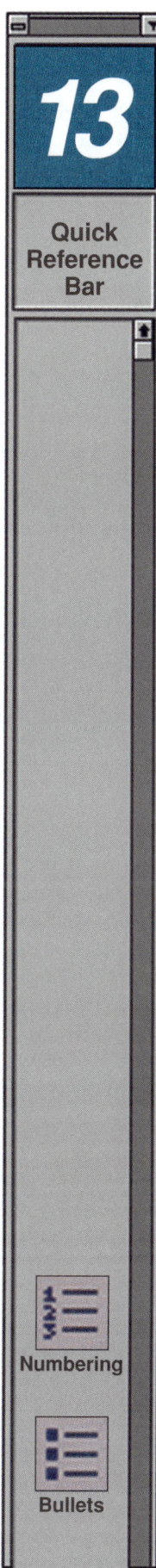

Numbering

Bullets

Formatting

14

❖ **Adding Borders and Shading**

With a few mouse clicks, you can add borders and/or shading to individual paragraphs in your document or to entire pages. The steps on this page describe how to work with the Borders and Shading dialog box. However, you can also issue most of the commands for adding borders and shading to paragraphs with the Tables and Borders toolbar (View, Toolbars, Tables and Borders).

1 Start Word and open Vacation Notes document from the My Documents folder.

2 Select all of the items in the bulleted list (don't include the heading *Notes for Housesitter* or any blank lines underneath the list), and choose Format, Borders and Shading to display the Borders and Shading dialog box.

> **ℹ** Because each item in a bulleted or numbered list is an individual paragraph, you need to select all of them before applying borders and shading. If you want to add borders and shading to a single paragraph, just click in it before issuing the command.

3 Click the Borders tab if necessary, and click Box under Setting. Then scroll down the Style list and click the double line. (If you like, you can also use the Color and Width drop-down lists to further adjust the appearance of the border.) The Preview area on the right side of the dialog box shows the border you've selected.

> **ℹ** If you want to use a variety of lines in your border, click Custom under Setting, choose a line style under Style, and then click the button for the border you want to affect in the Preview area.

4 Click the Shading tab and click the Gray-10% color in the Fill palette (the fourth color from the left in the first row). Then click OK.

> **ℹ** To remove borders, select the affected paragraphs (or click in a single paragraph), choose Format, Borders and Shading, and click None under Setting in the Border tab to remove all of the borders, or click individual buttons in the Preview area to remove just those borders. To remove shading, click the Shading tab and click None under Fill. Then click OK.

5 Word applies the borders and shading to your bulleted list. Click once to deselect the text. Point to the top border, and drag upward slightly to increase the distance between the border and the text inside the border. Then drag the bottom border downward slightly. (You can adjust the left and right borders in the same way.)

> **ℹ** To apply a border around the entire page, click the Page Border tab in the Borders and Shading dialog box. The border you select is by default added to all of the pages in your document. To add it to the first page only, choose This Section - First Page Only from the Apply To drop-down list. To apply the border to some pages and not others, divide your document into *sections* (see "Using Section Breaks"), and then specify the desired option in the Apply To drop-down list.

6 Save and close the document, and then close Word.

> **ℹ** To quickly add a horizontal border to your document, click the line above which you want to place the border, type —- (three hyphens), and press Enter. If you want a double-line border, type === (three equal signs). You can also try typing *** (three asterisks), ~~~ (three tildes), or ### (three pound signs) to create fancier lines. To enable or disable this feature, choose Tools, AutoCorrect, click the AutoFormat As You Type tab, mark or clear the Borders check box, and click OK.

Formatting

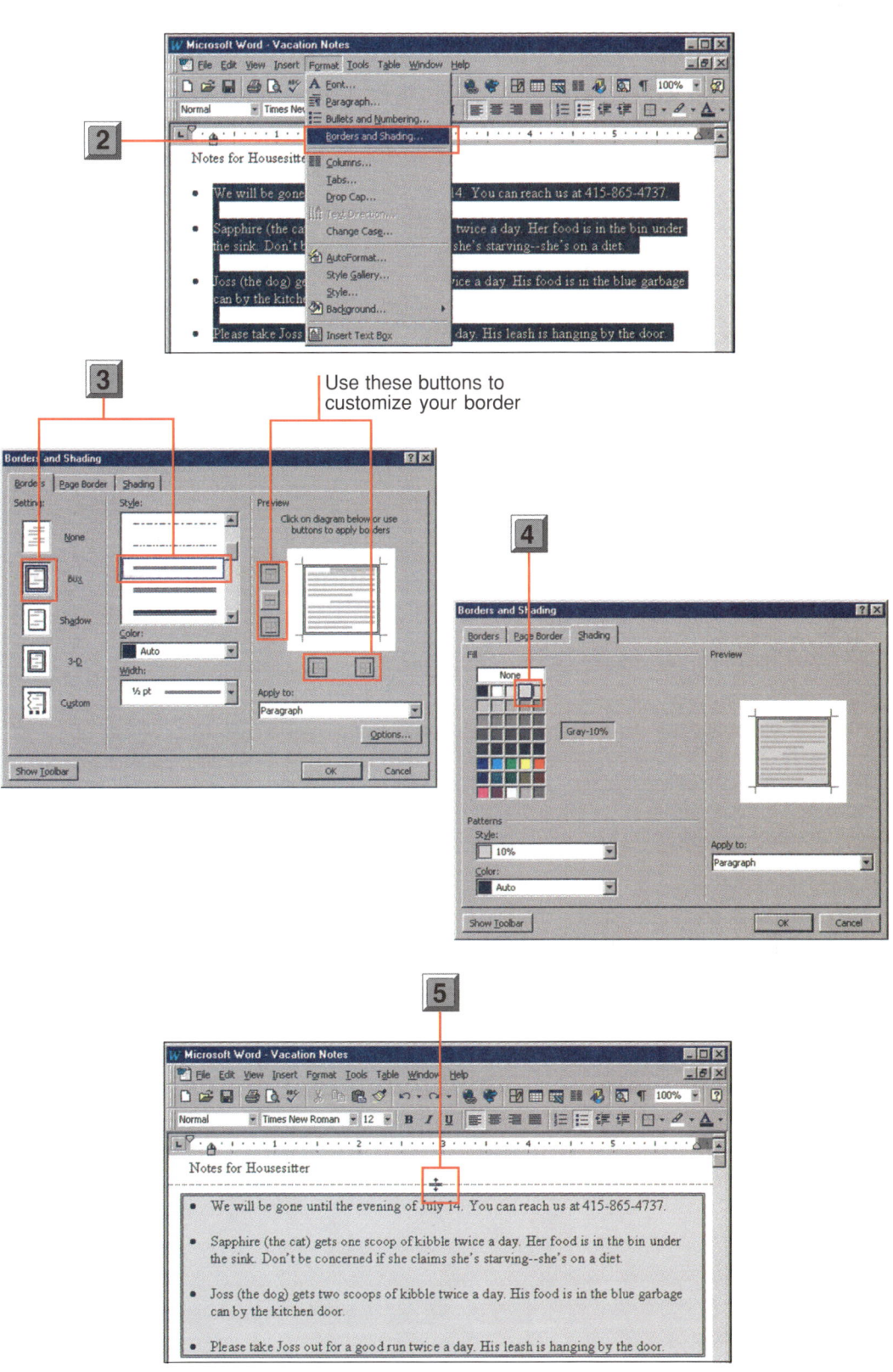

Use these buttons to
customize your border

Formatting

❖ Changing Margins, Paper Size, and Orientation

Word assumes that you want to print on 8˝-by-11-inch paper in portrait (vertical) orientation with 1 inch top and bottom margins and 1.25-inch left and right margins. These standard settings are fine most of the time, but you might need to change them occasionally. Margins, paper size, and orientation are page formatting features—that is, changing these settings automatically affects every page of the document. For this reason, it doesn't matter where the insertion point is when you make the formatting changes.

1 Start Word, and open the Reply to Sanders letter.

2 Choose File, Page Setup to display the Page Setup dialog box.

Changing margins

3 Click the Margins tab if it isn't already in front. If the value in the Top text box isn't already selected, double-click it to select it now. Then type over it with **1.5**.

4 Press the Tab key once to select the contents of the Bottom text box, and type **1.5**. Leave the left and right margins set to 1.25 inches.

> **ⓘ** If you are using Normal view, you won't see changes to the top and bottom margins on your screen. However, if you switch to Page Layout view (View, Page Layout) you can see these changes because this view provides a vertical ruler.

Changing paper size and orientation

5 Click the Paper Size tab. If your paper is a standard size (Legal, Executive, and so on), you can select it from the Paper Size drop-down list. If not, you need to type its width and height in the Width and Height text boxes. You can also change the orientation of the page so that text prints across the length of the page instead of the width. To do this, you would click the Landscape option button. Click OK to close the Page Setup dialog box without making any changes in the Paper Size tab.

6 If you like, click the Print button in the Standard toolbar to print a copy of the document. (You'll learn more about printing later in this book.)

7 Close the document without saving the changes, and then close Word.

> **ⓘ** If you want to use different page formatting on different pages in a document (print only one page of a 10-page document in landscape orientation for example), you need to insert section breaks. See "Using Section Breaks" later in this book for more information.

Formatting

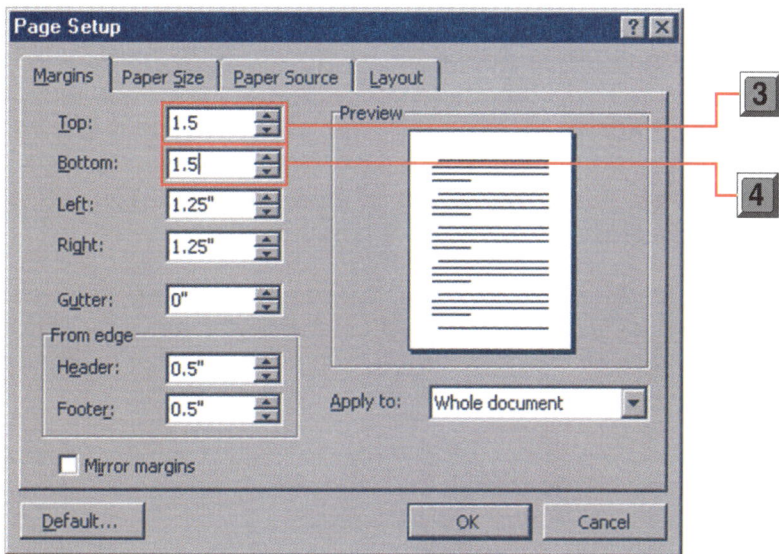

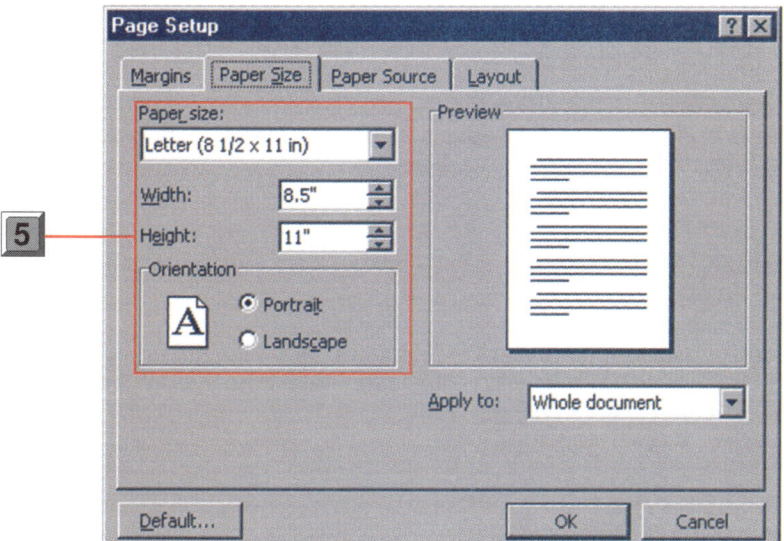

Editing and Proofing

❖ **Inserting and Deleting Text**

When you insert text into a document, Word normally pushes existing text to the right, and adjusts the line breaks to accommodate the new text. But you can also switch to overtype mode, so that each character you type replaces the character to the right of the insertion point. Besides explaining these two ways of inserting text, this lesson shows you three ways of deleting text. You learn how to delete characters, words, and entire blocks of text.

Inserting text

1 Start Word and open the Reply to Sanders letter from the My Documents folder. Click just before the word *discussion* in the paragraph that begins *As you will recall*, and type **phone** followed by a space. Word pushes the text to right to make room for the new word, and adjusts the line breaks.

2 Double-click the Overtype indicator (labeled OVR) at the right end of the status bar to turn it black. This enables overtype mode.

3 Click at the beginning of the paragraph beginning with *Thank you for your interest*, and type **We thank you for inquiring about our products**. The existing text is deleted as you type. Now double-click the Overtype indicator again to get out of overtype mode (it will become dim).

Deleting text

4 Use the Delete key and the Backspace key to delete one character at a time. The Delete key deletes the character to the right of the insertion point, and the Backspace key deletes the character to the left. Click just before the words *or Tuesday* and press Delete repeatedly to delete the two words and the space after them. Then click just after the word *product* at the end of the same paragraph and press Backspace repeatedly to delete the word *product* and the space before it.

5 Press Ctrl+Delete to delete the word to the right of the insertion point or Ctrl+Backspace to delete the word to the left. Click just before *on Monday*, hold down the Ctrl key, and press Delete twice to delete both words.

6 If you want to delete a large block of text, select it first, and then press the Delete key. Select from the start of the paragraph beginning with *In the meantime* through the price list and the blank line below it, and then press Delete.

> ⓘ If you want to replace one block of text with another, select the existing block of text, and then simply begin typing the new text; it will automatically replace the selected text.

7 Close the document without saving your changes, and then close Word.

Editing and Proofing

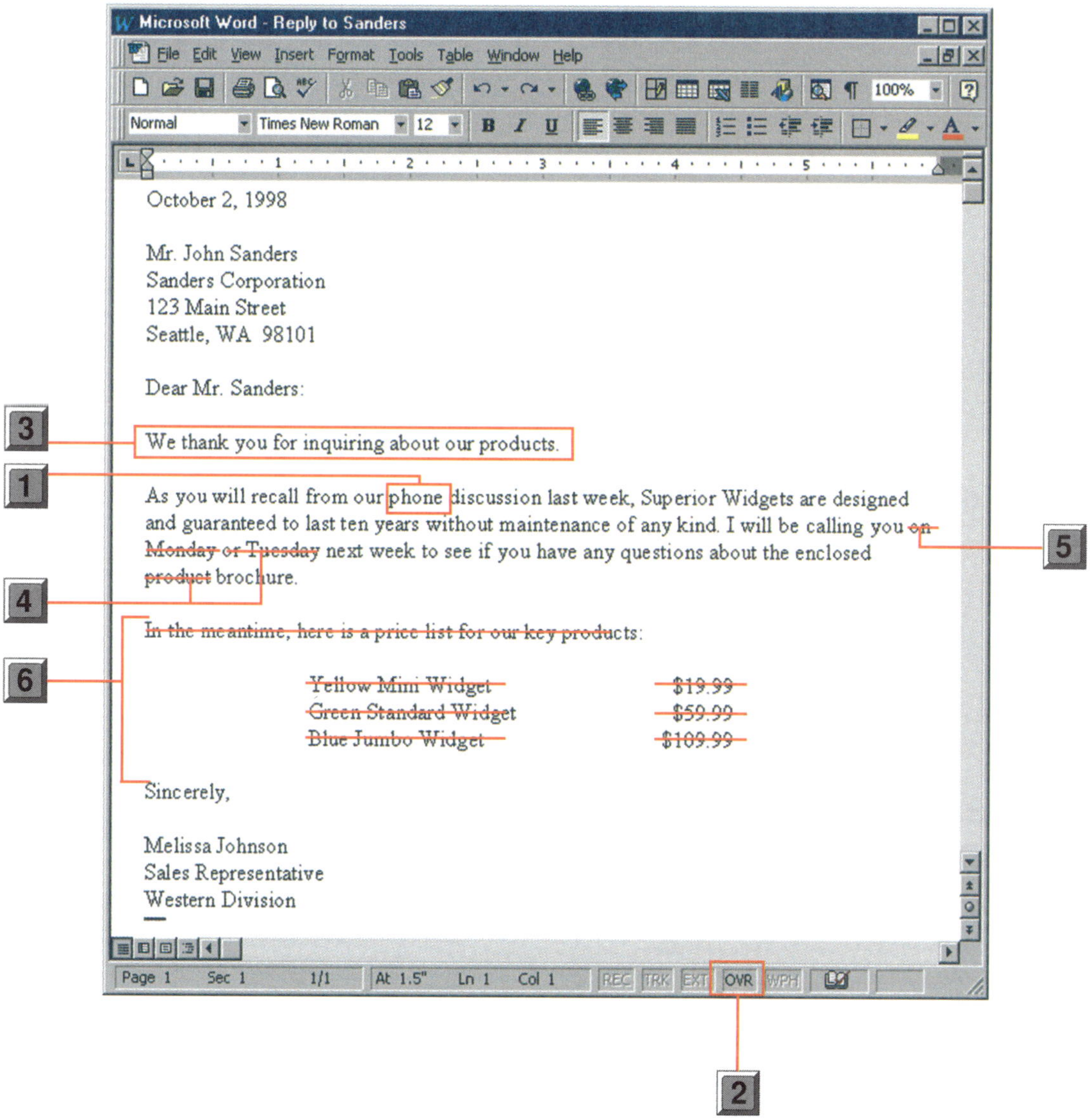

Microsoft Word - Reply to Sanders

File Edit View Insert Format Tools Table Window Help

Normal ▾ Times New Roman ▾ 12 ▾ **B** *I* U

October 2, 1998

Mr. John Sanders
Sanders Corporation
123 Main Street
Seattle, WA 98101

Dear Mr. Sanders:

[3] → We thank you for inquiring about our products.

[1] → As you will recall from our phone discussion last week, Superior Widgets are designed
and guaranteed to last ten years without maintenance of any kind. I will be calling you on ← **[5]**
Monday or Tuesday next week to see if you have any questions about the enclosed
product brochure.

[4] → In the meantime, here is a price list for our key products:

[6]
Yellow Mini Widget	$19.99
Green Standard Widget	$59.99
Blue Jumbo Widget	$109.99

Sincerely,

Melissa Johnson
Sales Representative
Western Division

Page 1   Sec 1   1/1   At 1.5"   Ln 1   Col 1   REC TRK EXT **OVR** WPH

[2]

Editing and Proofing

❖ Working with Multiple Open Documents

Word lets you open more than one document and switch back and forth between them. This comes in handy when you're creating one document and using another as a reference, or when you need to copy information from one document to another (see the next lesson).

1 Start Word, and type the following text, *making sure* to type all of the spelling and grammatical mistakes as shown. (You'll use this document in "Correcting Spelling and Grammar" later in this book.) Then save the document in the My Documents folder with the name Casual Day.

MEMORANDUM

Date: November 14, 1998
To: All Staff
From: Janet Stevenson

Starting next month, Fridays will be designated casaul days. On these days, your welcome to wear casual clothes instead of of your regular business attire. If you have a questions about this, please let me know.

---

2 Without closing the memo, click the New button in the Standard toolbar and type the incomplete document shown below. (You'll finish it in the next lesson.) Save it in the My Documents folder with the name Pricing Info.

Hi Terry:

Here is the pricing information you asked for:

Please let me know if you need anything else.
John

---

3 Leave both new documents open, and open the Reply to Sanders letter.

4 Display the Window menu. All three documents are listed at the bottom of the menu. Reply to Sanders has a check mark next to it because it is on top. The other two are hidden behind it. Click Casual Day to switch to that document.

5 Display the Window menu again and this time click Pricing Info.

6 Press Ctrl+F6 repeatedly. This keyboard shortcut lets you cycle through all of your open documents.

7 Close all three documents, and then and close Word.

> ℹ Although you don't have to save a document before switching to another one, it's prudent to do so. That way, if you lose power while multiple documents are open, you won't lose any changes in the documents that are hidden.

Editing and Proofing

Quick Reference Bar

Press Ctrl+F6 to switch between open documents

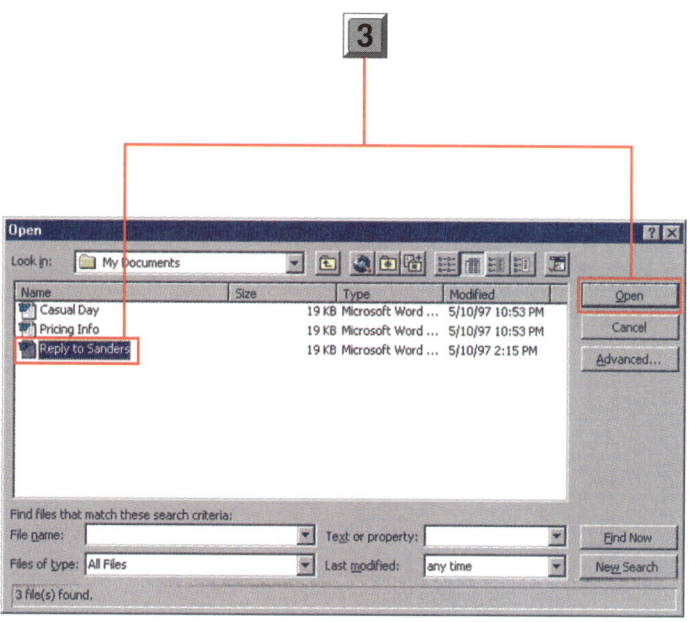

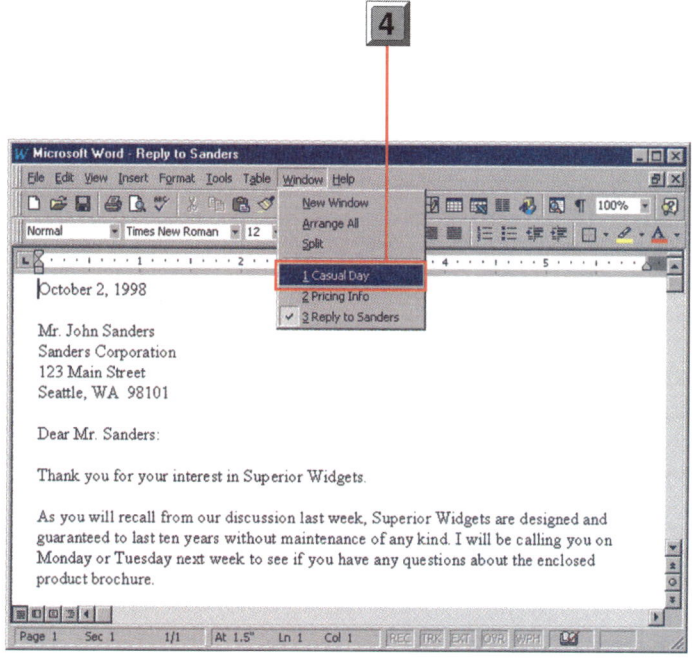

Editing and Proofing

❖ Moving and Copying Text

While editing documents, you will inevitably need to move (cut) some blocks of text. You might need to rearrange some sentences in a paragraph, or move a paragraph from one location to another. You can also copy text, leaving it in its original location and putting a duplicate somewhere else. Word supplies two methods of moving and copying text. One method—using the Cut, Copy, and Paste commands—lets you cut and copy text within a document, between documents, or between Word and other programs. A second method, drag-and-drop, provides a fast and intuitive way of moving or copying text a short distance within a document.

Using Cut, Copy, and Paste

1 Start Word, and open the Reply to Sanders letter. Select the sentence beginning *As you will recall*, and then click Cut button in the Standard toolbar (or choose Edit, Cut). The sentence is removed from the document and placed in the Windows Clipboard (a temporary storage area used to hold information that's being cut or copied between Windows applications).

2 Click just past the sentence ending with *product brochure.*, and click the Paste button in the Standard toolbar (or choose Edit, Paste). The two sentences in the paragraph are now reversed.

3 Select all three lines in the price list, as well as the blank line underneath them, and click the Copy button in the Standard toolbar (or choose Edit, Copy). Word leaves the text in the document, and places a copy of it on the Windows Clipboard.

4 Open the Pricing Info document you created in the previous lesson (you saved it in the My Documents folder). Click at the beginning of the sentence that starts with *Please let me know*. Click the Paste button in the Standard toolbar to paste the price list from the Reply to Sanders letter. Save and close Pricing Info, and then display the Window menu and click Reply to Sanders to switch back to that document.

5 Click once to deselect the text you just copied into Pricing Info. Then select the word *Yellow* in the price list, point to it, and drag to just before the word *Widget*. A dotted insertion point shows where the text will be pasted when you release the mouse button, and a small square is now attached to the mouse pointer.

Using drag-and-drop

6 When you release the mouse button, the text is pasted into the new location. Drag the words *Green* and *Blue* just past the words *Standard* and *Jumbo*, respectively. Then close Reply to Sanders without saving the changes, and exit Word.

 If you want to copy instead of move text when you use drag-and-drop, hold down the Ctrl key as you are dragging the text to the new location. When you do this, Word adds a small plus sign to the mouse pointer to indicate that you are performing a copy operation. Make sure you release the mouse button *before* releasing the Ctrl key, otherwise you'll move instead of copying the selected text.

Editing and Proofing

1

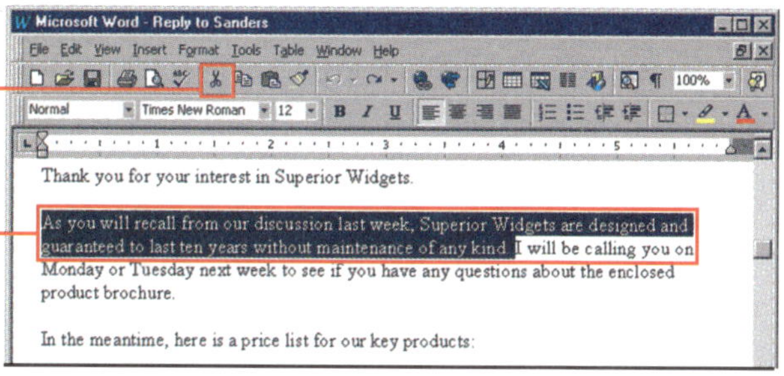

Thank you for your interest in Superior Widgets.

As you will recall from our discussion last week, Superior Widgets are designed and guaranteed to last ten years without maintenance of any kind. I will be calling you on Monday or Tuesday next week to see if you have any questions about the enclosed product brochure.

In the meantime, here is a price list for our key products:

2

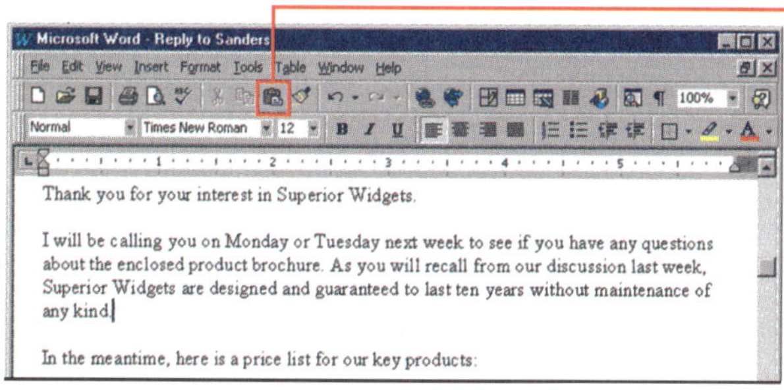

Thank you for your interest in Superior Widgets.

I will be calling you on Monday or Tuesday next week to see if you have any questions about the enclosed product brochure. As you will recall from our discussion last week, Superior Widgets are designed and guaranteed to last ten years without maintenance of any kind.

In the meantime, here is a price list for our key products:

3

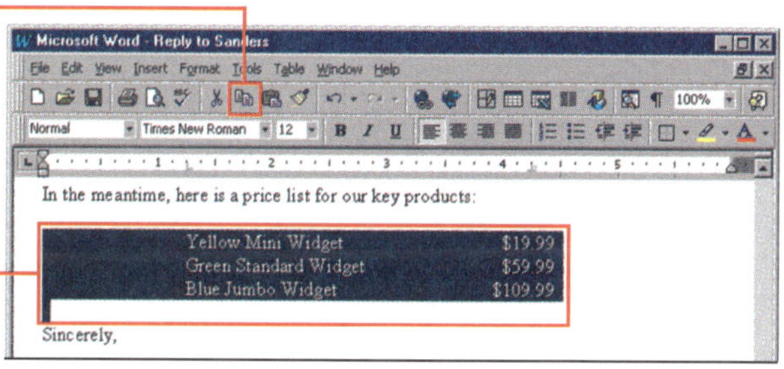

In the meantime, here is a price list for our key products:

Yellow Mini Widget	$19.99
Green Standard Widget	$59.99
Blue Jumbo Widget	$109.99

Sincerely,

4

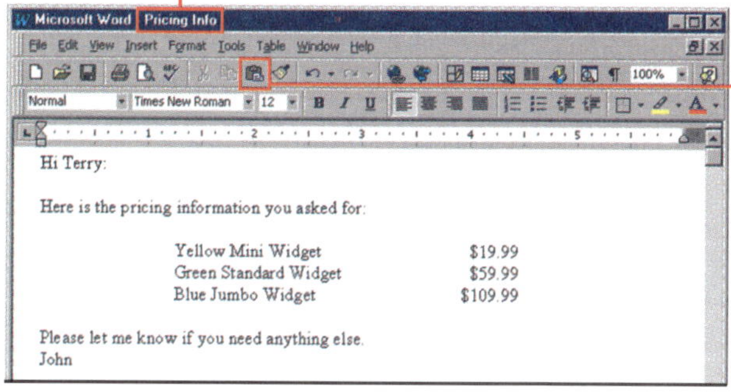

Hi Terry:

Here is the pricing information you asked for:

Yellow Mini Widget	$19.99
Green Standard Widget	$59.99
Blue Jumbo Widget	$109.99

Please let me know if you need anything else.
John

5

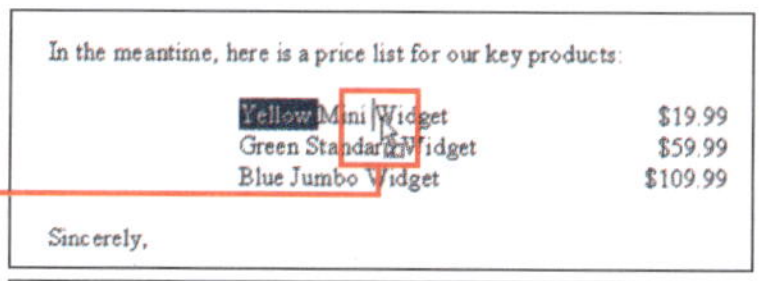

In the meantime, here is a price list for our key products:

Yellow Mini Widget	$19.99
Green Standard Widget	$59.99
Blue Jumbo Widget	$109.99

Sincerely,

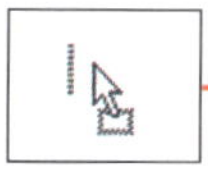

Drag-and-drop cut pointer

6

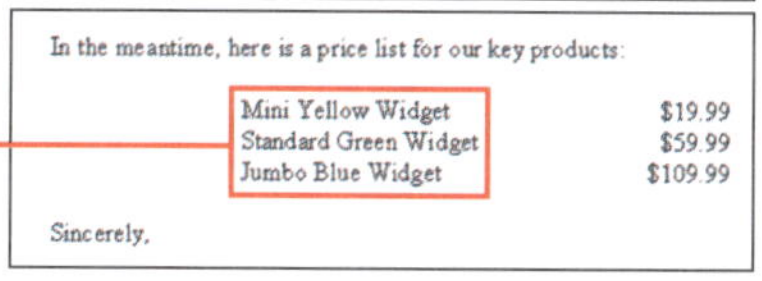

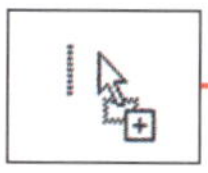

In the meantime, here is a price list for our key products:

Mini Yellow Widget	$19.99
Standard Green Widget	$59.99
Jumbo Blue Widget	$109.99

Sincerely,

Drag-and-drop copy pointer

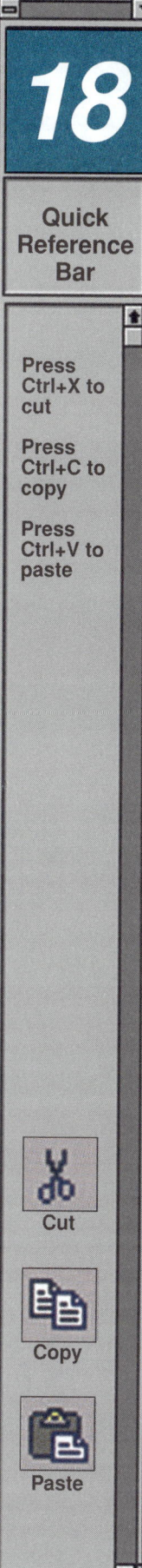

Quick Reference Bar

Press Ctrl+X to cut

Press Ctrl+C to copy

Press Ctrl+V to paste

Cut

Copy

Paste

Editing and Proofing

❖ Using AutoCorrect

If you're like the rest of us, you make certain typing and spelling errors over and over. Word's AutoCorrect feature fixes these types of mistakes automatically. You can also use AutoCorrect entries as shortcuts for typing symbols, long names, or phrases. AutoCorrect already knows how to correct many misspelled words; in this lesson, you learn how to add entries to the list. The entries you create will be available in all documents.

1 Start Word, and choose Tools, AutoCorrect to display the AutoCorrect dialog box. Click the AutoCorrect tab if it isn't already in front, and scroll through the list at the bottom of the dialog box to see what AutoCorrect already knows how to fix. When you type any entry in the left column, Word automatically replaces it with the corresponding entry in the right column. The top of the list contains shortcuts for inserting various symbols. (For example, if you type *(tm)*, Word automatically replaces it with the trademark symbol ™.) Further down the list are many commonly misspelled words.

> ⓘ The top part of the AutoCorrect tab contains check boxes for options that fix common typing mistakes. You can pick and choose which of these options you want to use, but make sure to keep the Replace Text As You Type check box marked. Otherwise, AutoCorrect won't fix your mistakes.

2 Click in the Replace text box and type the misspelled word **leprechon**. Then press the Tab key to move into the With text box, and type the correct spelling **leprechaun**.

> ⓘ You cannot include a space at the end of an entry in the Replace text box. However, you can include spaces between words. For example, you could type **int he** in the Replace text box and **in the** in the With text box.

3 Click the Add button to add the entry to the list, and then click the OK button.

4 To test the entry, type **She saw a leprechon** and press the Spacebar. Word immediately replaces the incorrect spelling with the correct one.

5 Choose Tools, AutoCorrect, and click in the Replace text box. This time, you'll create an entry that lets you quickly type a long name. Type **napf** in the Replace text box, and type **National Association of Parrot Fanciers** in the With text box. Click Add, and then click OK.

> ⓘ When you type an abbreviation in the Replace text box, make sure to use something that you don't want to actually leave "as is" in your documents. (For instance, don't use **bad** as an abbreviation for **Birdwatcher's Alliance of Dallas**.) Word will convert the abbreviation to the full spelling (the text you typed in the With text box) every time you type it.

6 Move to a new line in the document, type **Please contact the napf**, and press the Spacebar. Word automatically converts the abbreviation to the full spelling.

> ⓘ To delete an AutoCorrect entry, display the AutoCorrect dialog box and scroll through the list of entries to locate the one you want to delete. Click the entry, click the Delete button, and then click OK.

7 Close the document without saving (Word will save your AutoCorrect entries), and close Word.

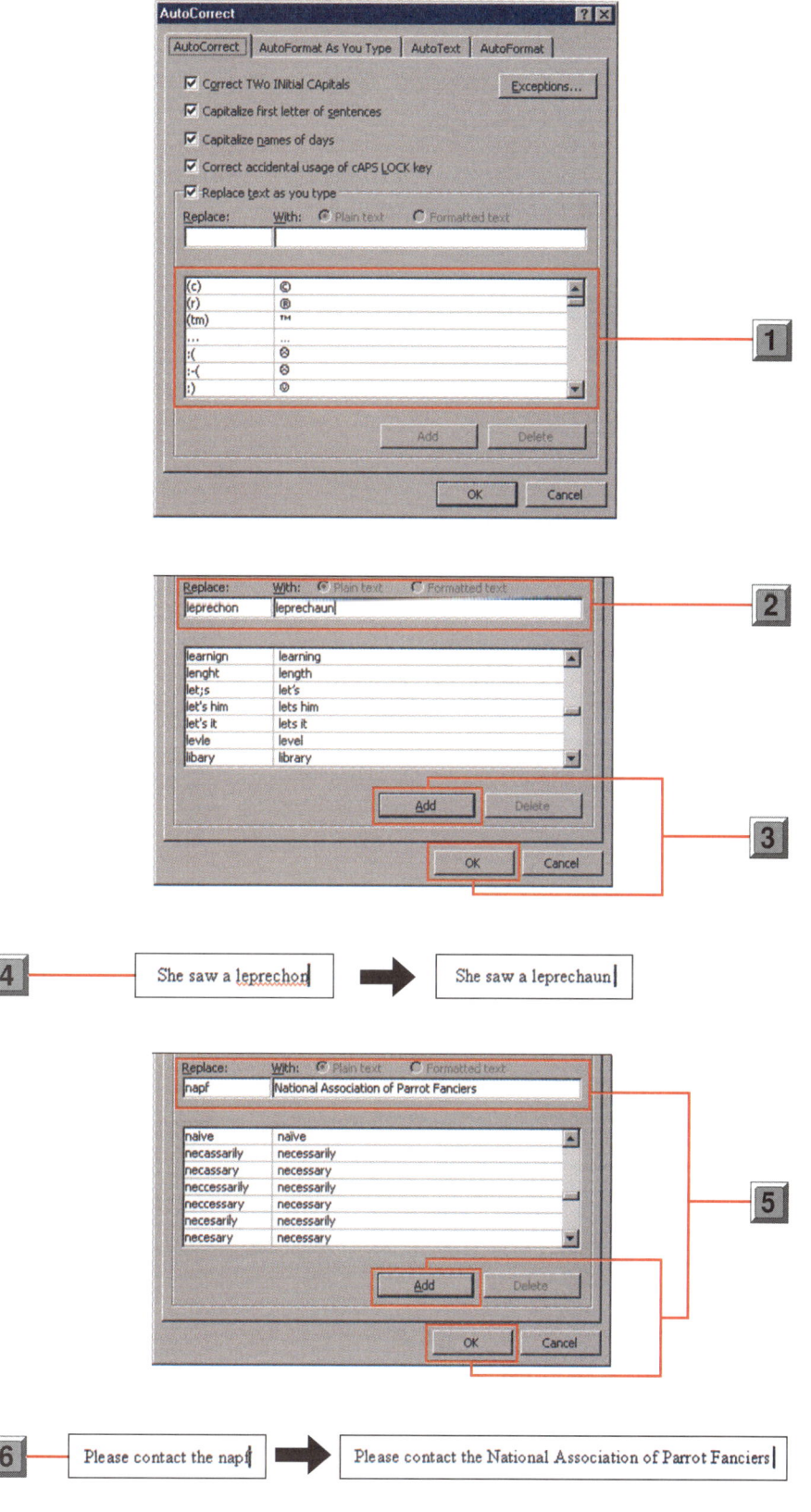

Editing and Proofing

20

❖ **Correcting Spelling and Grammar**

Word gives you two ways of correcting spelling and grammar. You can wait until you've finished typing your text, and then click the Spelling and Grammar button on the Standard toolbar (or choose Tools, Spelling and Grammar) to check the entire document. Or you can check spelling and grammar "on the fly" as you're working. This lesson explains how to use the second method.

1 Start Word, and open the Casual Day memo from the My Documents folder. (You created this memo in "Working with Multiple Open Documents" earlier in this book.)

2 Word places red wavy lines under words that might be misspelled and green wavy lines under words or phrases that might be grammatically incorrect. Right-click the misspelled word *casaul* to display a context menu of possible correct spellings, and click *casual* to fix the spelling.

> ℹ️ If a word marked with a red wavy line is spelled correctly and you use it frequently, click Add in the context menu to add it to the dictionary so that Word won't mark it in future documents. If the word is spelled correctly but you don't use it that often, you can choose Ignore All to prevent Word from marking the word in the current document without adding the word to the dictionary.

3 Now right-click on the word *your* with a green wavy line underneath it. Choose *you're* from the context menu to correct this grammatical error.

> ℹ️ If a word or phrase is marked with a green wavy line but you don't want to change it, you can hide the green wavy line by choosing Ignore Sentence from the context menu.

4 Right-click the second instance of the word *of*, and choose Delete Repeated Word from the context menu.

5 Right-click *atire*. This time, point to AutoCorrect in the context menu and choose *attire* in the submenu that appears. This creates an AutoCorrect entry for the misspelling. (See the previous lesson for more on AutoCorrect.) From now on, Word will make this correction for you.

6 Right-click *a questions*, choose *question* from the context menu, and then save and close the document before closing Word.

> ℹ️ If the wavy lines annoy you, you can hide or disable automatic spell and grammar checking. Choose Tools, Options, and click the Spelling & Grammar tab. Mark the Hide Spelling Errors in This Document check box if you want to temporarily hide the red wavy lines in the current document, and mark the Hide Grammatical Errors in This Document check box to hide the green wavy lines. If you don't want to use automatic spelling and grammar checking in *any* document, clear the check boxes labeled Check Spelling As You Type and Check Grammar As You Type. Then click OK.

Editing and Proofing

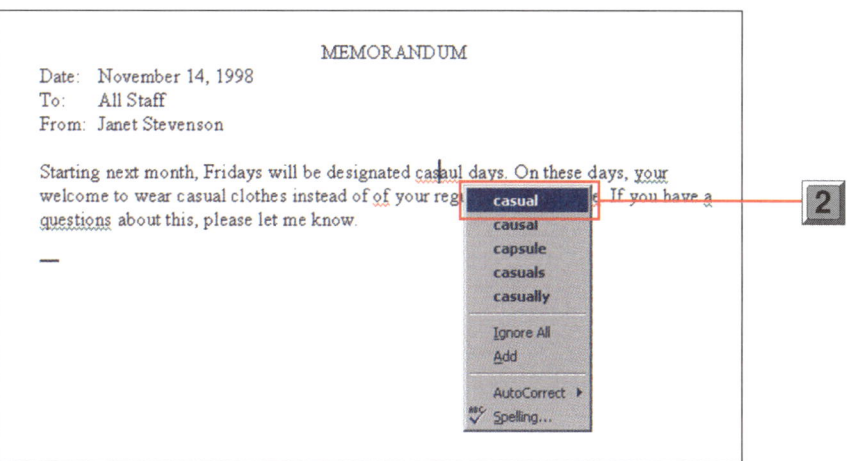

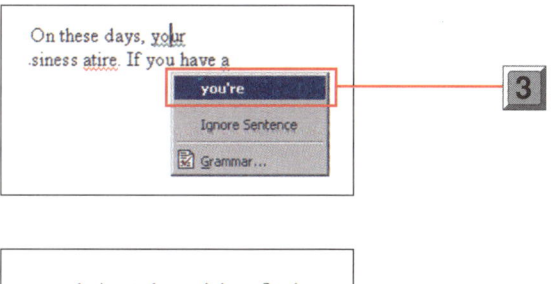

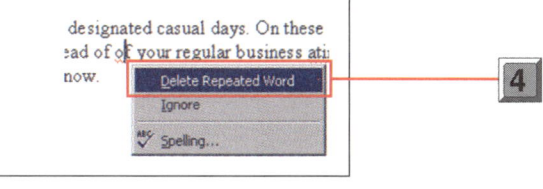

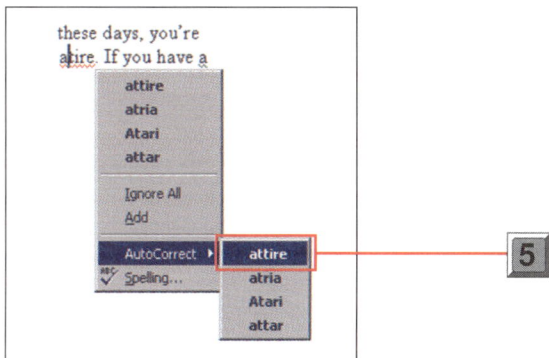

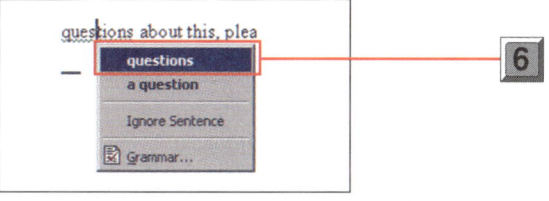

21 Printing

❖ Print Preview

Word lets you see what your printed document will look like before you actually send it to the printer. Using Print Preview is a great way to avoid wasting paper, because you can spot problems in your document before you print, not after.

1 Start Word, and open the Reply to Sanders letter from the My Documents folder.

2 Click the Print Preview button in the Standard toolbar (or choose File, Print Preview).

3 Word displays the letter in the Print Preview window. Click the One Page button in the Print Preview toolbar to view the full page at the largest magnification possible.

> ℹ️ There are two visual cues that you're using Print Preview: [Preview] appears in the title bar, and the Print Preview toolbar replaces the Standard and Formatting toolbars.

4 Click the Magnifier button in the Print Preview toolbar (if it isn't already selected). When you point to the page, the mouse pointer becomes a magnifying glass with a plus sign. (If you're viewing multiple pages and you don't see the magnifying glass, click once on the page you want to magnify and then the mouse pointer will change into a magnifying glass.) Click the price list in the letter.

5 The area enlarges, and the plus sign in the mouse pointer changes to a minus sign. Click the page again to shrink the page to its previous size.

6 Click the Close button in the middle of the Print Preview toolbar to close Print Preview.

> ℹ️ If your document is more than one page long, you can press the Page Up and Page Down keys while you're in Print Preview to view your document page by page. You can also view multiple pages at one time. To do this, click the Multiple Pages button in the Print Preview toolbar. A grid drops down with small squares that represent pages. Drag through the desired number of squares to select them. For example, to view four pages, drag through four squares. (The grid enlarges as you drag.)

7 If you're going on to the next lesson, leave the Reply to Sanders letter open. Otherwise, close the document and exit Word.

Printing

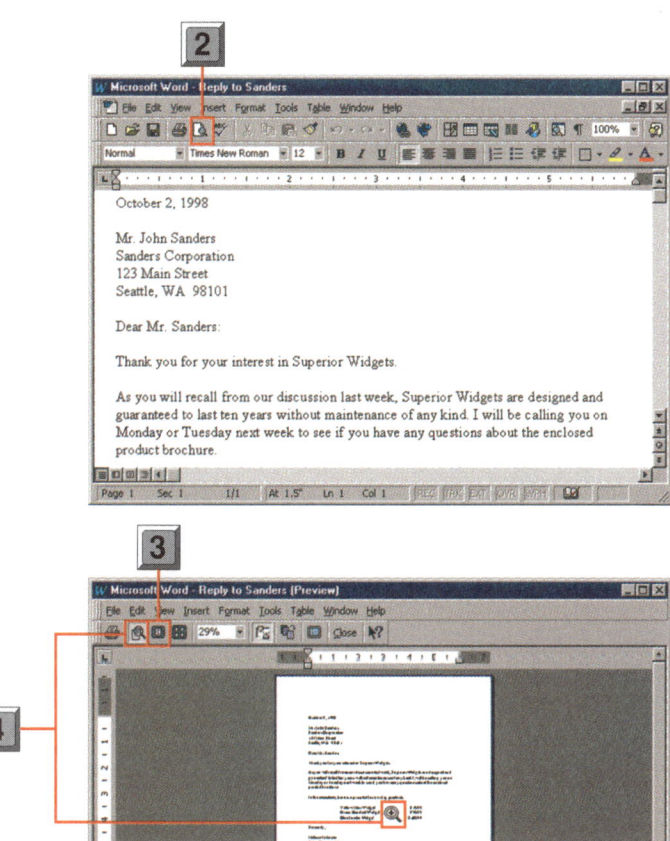

21

Press F2 to switch to and from Print Preview

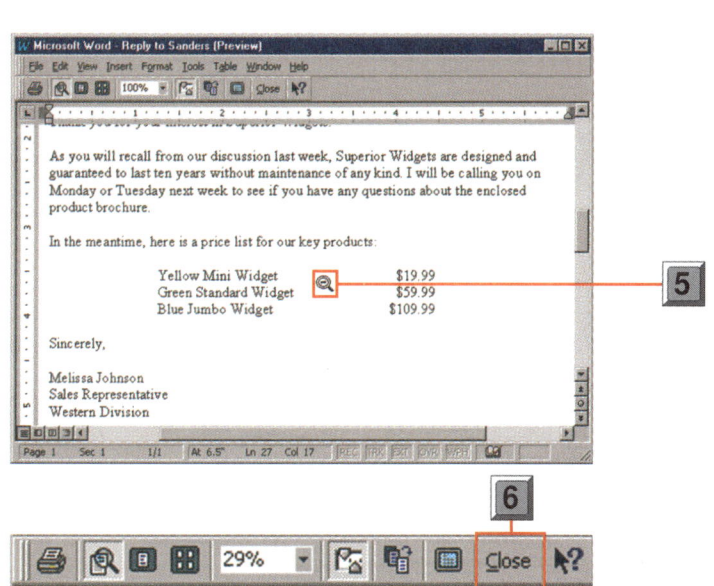

Print Preview

One Page

Magnifier

Multiple Pages

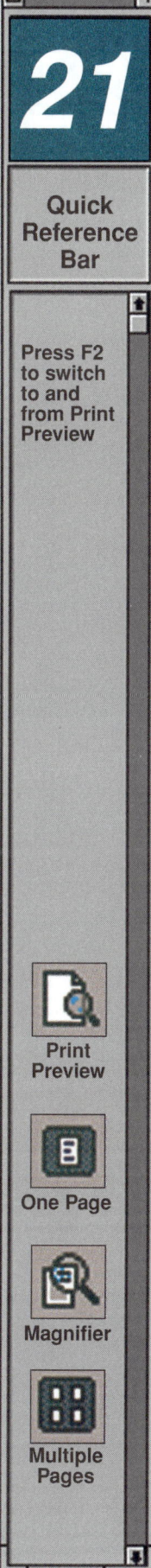

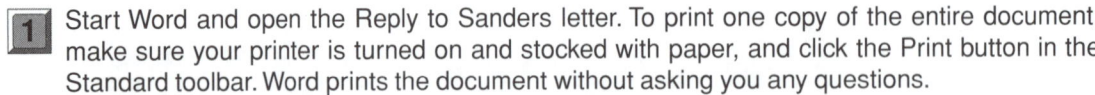

Printing

❖ Printing a Document

Word assumes that you usually want to print one complete copy of your document, so the Print toolbar button lets you do just that. If you need to customize your printing at all, you have to print from the Print dialog box instead. This lesson shows you both ways of printing.

1 Start Word and open the Reply to Sanders letter. To print one copy of the entire document, make sure your printer is turned on and stocked with paper, and click the Print button in the Standard toolbar. Word prints the document without asking you any questions.

> ℹ️ When you point to the Print button, a ToolTip lists what printer is currently selected. If you want to print to a different printer, choose File, Print, and choose the printer from among the installed printers in the Name drop-down list. Then click OK to print your document, or click Close to accept the new default printer and close the dialog box without printing. The printer you choose becomes the default printer for all Word documents until you choose a different printer from the Name drop-down list.

2 Select the three lines of the price list (from *Yellow Mini Widget* to *$109.99*), and then choose File, Print (or press Ctrl+P) to display the Print dialog box.

3 Click the Selection option button, and then click OK. Word prints only the selected text. This option button is dim (unavailable) unless you have selected text in your document.

4 Click once to deselect the text, and choose File, Print again. The value in the Number of Copies text box is already selected when the Print dialog box appears. Type over it with **2** to print two copies of the letter. If you actually want to print the document, click OK. Otherwise, click Cancel.

5 Close the document without saving any changes, and then close Word.

> ℹ️ Word offers two options for specifying which pages of a multiple-page document to print. If you only want to print one page, move the insertion point to that page before you display the Print dialog box, and then click the Current Page option button before clicking OK. If you want to print some but not all of the pages, display the Print dialog box, and type the range of pages in the Pages text box before clicking OK. Use hyphens to separate sequential page ranges, and commas to separate nonsequential pages. For example, you could type 3-5, 8, 17-19 to print pages 3, 4, 5, 8, 17, 18, and 19 of a 20-page document.

Printing

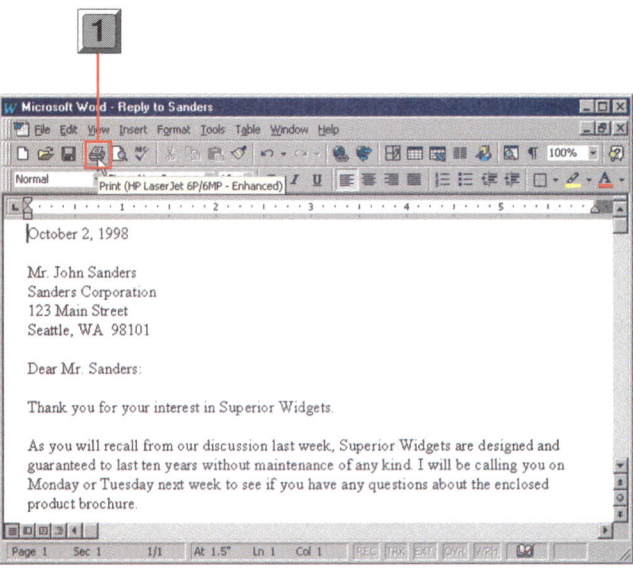

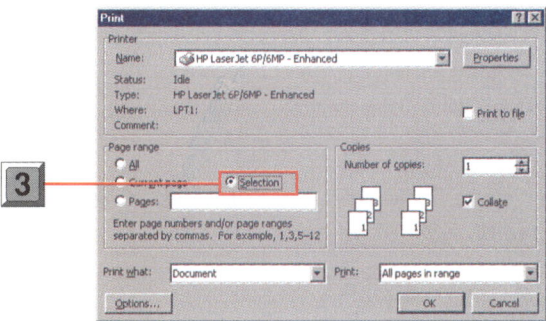

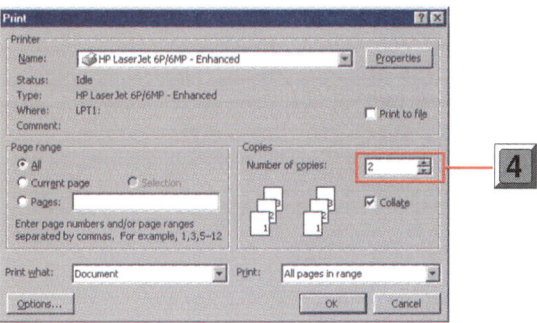

22

23 | *Printing*

❖ Printing an Envelope

In Word, the process of printing envelopes is so streamlined that it's largely self-explanatory. Word knows the dimensions of all of the standard envelope sizes, and places the return address and delivery address in the proper positions on the envelope. If the letter you are sending is on your screen, Word knows how to locate the delivery address at the top of the letter.

1 Start Word, and open the Reply to Sanders letter.

2 Choose Tools, Envelopes and Labels to display the Envelopes and Labels dialog box.

3 Click the Envelopes tab if it isn't already in front. Word automatically places the delivery address from the letter in the Delivery Address text box. You can edit the address if you like, although in this exercise, you don't need to.

4 If you entered your own mailing address in the User Information tab of the Options dialog box (see "Customizing Word" earlier in this book), it appears in the Return Address text box. If necessary, you can edit the return address now.

> ℹ️ If you edit the return address, Word asks whether you want to save the new address as the default return address. If you click Yes, Word enters the address in the User Information tab of the Options dialog box and uses the new address in future envelopes.

5 If your envelope has a preprinted return address, you can mark the Omit check box to keep Word from printing the return address. Leave the check box clear for this lesson.

6 Load an envelope in your printer. If you aren't sure how to load envelopes, look in your printer manual. This varies from printer to printer.

> ℹ️ Word assumes you want to print a standard business envelope. If your envelope is a different size, you can click the Options button to display the Envelope Options dialog box, choose a different envelope size in the Envelope Size drop-down list, and click OK.

7 Click the Print button. Then close the document without saving changes, and exit Word.

> ℹ️ If you like, you can click the Add to Document button instead of the Print button to add the envelope to the top of your document. Do this if you want to print the envelope every time you print the document. Make sure to have an envelope loaded in your printer before you print a document that contains an envelope because the envelope prints as the first page.

Printing

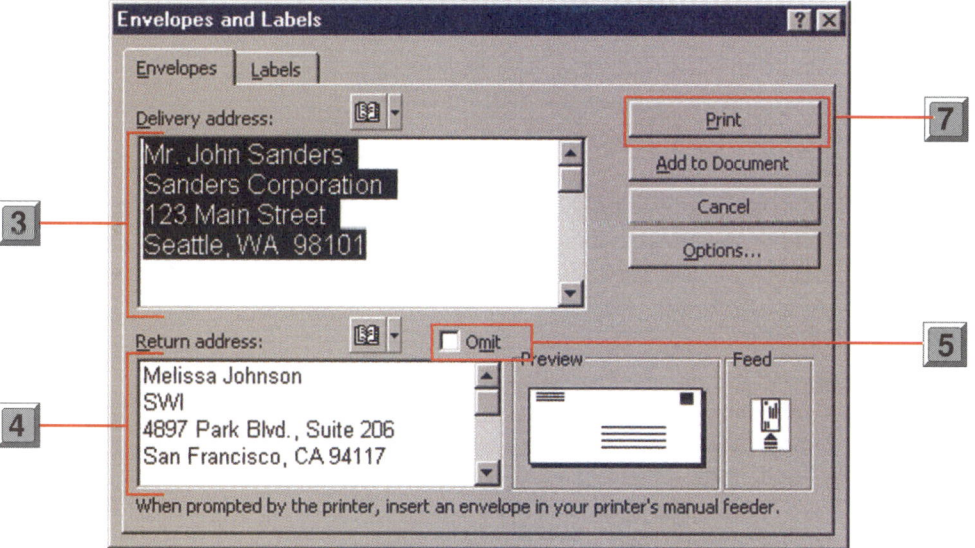

Typing Timesavers

24

❖ **Entering the Date Automatically**

Instead of typing the current date yourself, you can ask Word to get the date from the computer's clock and insert it for you. You can also insert the date as a field. If you do this, Word updates the date to the current day's date each time you open the document.

1 Start Word. Or, if you already have a document open in Word, start a new document. Type the letter shown on the facing page, pressing Enter twice at the top of the document to create two blank lines. Then save it in the My Documents folder under the name Sorry Harry.

2 Press Ctrl+Home to move to the top of the letter, and start typing the current month. After you type the first few letters, Word displays an AutoComplete tip containing the full name of the month. Ignore this tip, finish typing the month, and then add a space. As soon as you do, Word displays an AutoComplete tip suggesting the current date. Press Enter to let Word complete the date for you.

> ℹ️ If AutoComplete isn't working, choose Insert, AutoText, AutoText; make sure the AutoText tab is in front; mark the check box labeled Show AutoComplete Tip for AutoText and Dates; and then click OK. AutoComplete inserts the date as text. If you want to insert it as a field, use the Date and Time dialog box or the keyboard shortcut, as described in the remaining steps.

3 Delete the date you just inserted, keep your insertion point at the beginning of the document, and choose Insert, Date and Time to display the Date and Time dialog box. Mark the Update Automatically check box to insert the date as a field. (If you don't mark this box, Word inserts the date as normal text, just as if you had typed it yourself.) Then select the third format, click the Default button, and click Yes when Word confirms that you want to change the default date format. Finally, click OK to close the dialog box. (Word uses the format that you set as the default when you insert the date with a keyboard shortcut, as described in step 6 below.)

4 Click the date in the letter. It turns a light shade of gray to indicate that it is a field, not standard text. If you save this document today and open it tomorrow, the date will automatically update to tomorrow's date.

> ℹ️ If you insert a date as a field and then decide that you don't want it to update automatically, you can convert it to normal text. To do this, click inside the date and press Ctrl+Shift+F9. Then click anywhere to deselect the date.

5 Drag across the date field to select it. (It will appear as white text on a gray background.) Then press the Delete key to delete it. It's easiest to delete fields if you select them first.

6 Now press Alt+Shift+D to insert the date a final time. Word uses the format you chose in step 3.

7 Save the letter again, and then close it and exit from Word.

> ℹ️ If Word's automatic date feature inserts the wrong date, your computer's clock is not set correctly. Double-click the time at the right end of the Windows 95 taskbar, choose the date and time in the Date/Time Properties dialog box, and click OK.

Typing Timesavers

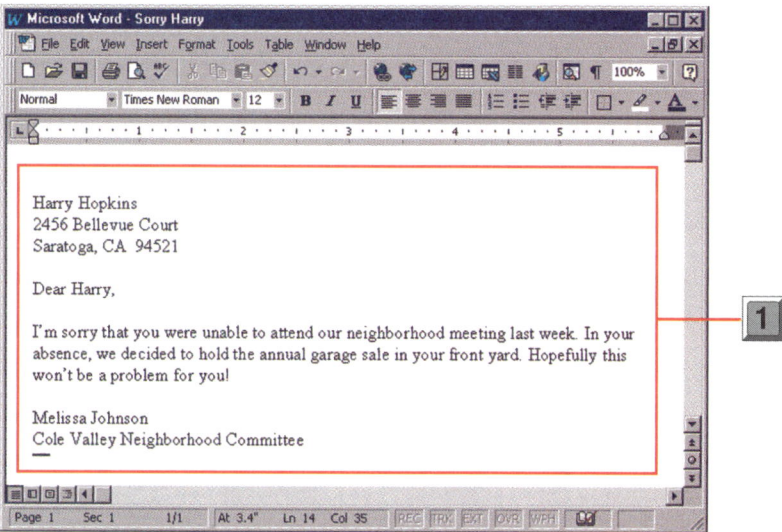

Press Alt+Shift +D to insert the date

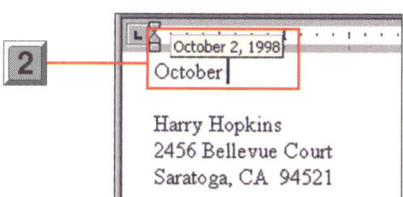

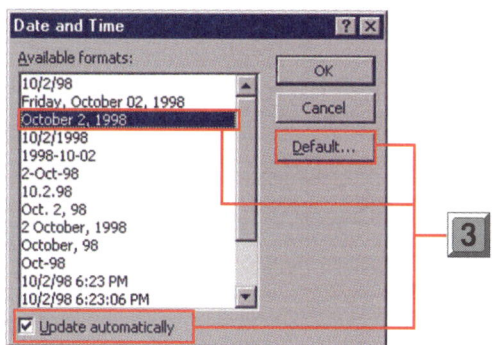

Typing Timesavers

❖ **Using Find and Replace**

Word's find feature can search a document of any length for a word or phrase, or even for formatting or symbols such as tabs and paragraph marks. And if you need to replace the found text with something else, the replace feature can get the job done quickly.

1 Start Word, type the paragraph shown in the figure on the facing page, and then press Ctrl+Home.

Using find

2 Choose Edit, Find (or press Ctrl+F) to display the Find tab of the Find and Replace dialog box. Type **puppy** in the Find What box, and then click Find Next.

3 Word highlights the first occurrence of the word *puppy*. Keep clicking Find Next until Word displays a message box telling you that it has finished searching the document. Click OK, and then click Cancel to close the Find and Replace dialog box.

Using replace

4 Press Ctrl+Home to move back to the beginning of the document. Then choose Edit, Replace (or press Ctrl+H) to display the Replace tab of the Find and Replace dialog box. This time, you'll replace all instances of *puppy* with *lamb*. (For the uninitiated, the term *lamb clip* is synonymous with *puppy clip* in the world of poodle grooming.) The word **puppy** should still be in the Find What box. Type **lamb** in the Replace With box. Then click Find Next.

5 Word highlights the first instance of the word *puppy*. Click Replace to replace just this one instance of *puppy* with *lamb*. When Word highlights the next matching word, click Replace All to replace both the highlighted word and the rest of the matching words in the document. Click OK when a message box informs you that Word has finished searching the document and made two replacements. (It only reports the number of replacements Word made after you clicked the Replace All button.)

6 Click the More button to expand the dialog box. This button displays the same options in both the Find tab and the Replace tab.

7 Use Match Case to find only occurrences of the search text that have the same combination of upper- and lowercase letters you typed in the Find What box. Use Find Whole Words Only if you don't want Word to find the search text when it's part of another word—for instance, if you only want to find the word *cat,* not *catch, decathlon,* or *scathing.*

8 Use Wildcards lets you use wildcard characters in the Find What text. You can type them bad break directly, or click the Special button and choose them from a list. (If you aren't sure what a wildcard is, use the Office Assistant to search for information on Find and Replace.) Sounds Like finds text that sounds like the search text; use this option if you're not sure of the spelling. Find All Word Forms finds all forms of the word: If you search for *sing,* Word will also find *sings, sang, sung,* and *singing.*

9 Click the Less button to collapse the dialog box and then click the Close button to close it. Close the document without saving, and exit from Word.

ℹ The Format and Special buttons—available if you click the More button in the Find and Replace dialog box—let you perform more sophisticated find/replace operations. Use the Format button while the insertion point is in the Find What or Replace With box to specify formatting that you want to find and/or replace. Use the Special button to indicate symbols such as tabs and paragraph marks you want to find and/or replace.

Typing Timesavers

1

Poodles that are kept as pets and not show dogs are usually groomed in one of two styles: *puppy* and *sporting*. Similar in appearance, these clips both trim the coat over most of the body and closely shave the hair on the feet, tail, face, and neck. The coat in a puppy clip is usually kept longer and shaped, while it's cut quite short in a sporting clip. Pompons decorate the end of the tail in both the puppy clip and the sporting clip, and the sporting clip may have ankle ruffs.

Press Ctrl+F to display the Find tab of the Find and Replace dialog box

Press Ctrl+H to display the Replace tab of the Find and Replace dialog box

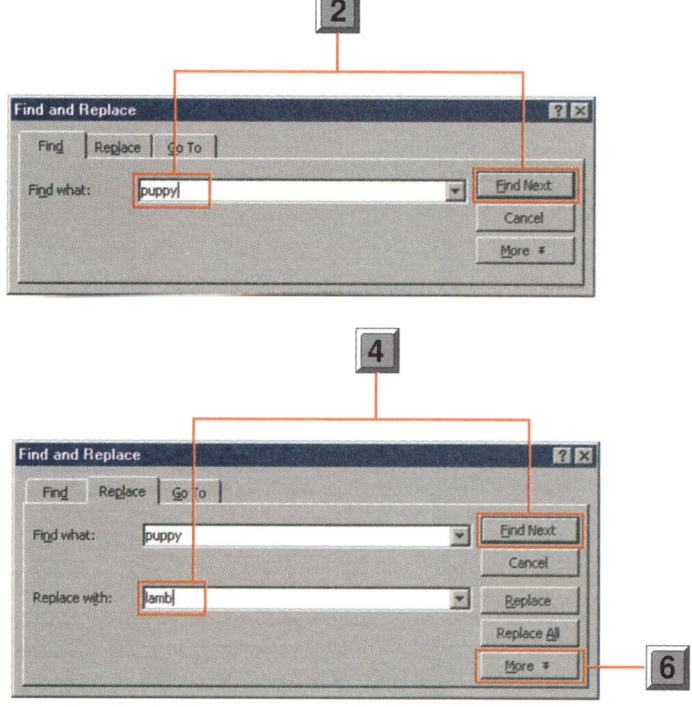

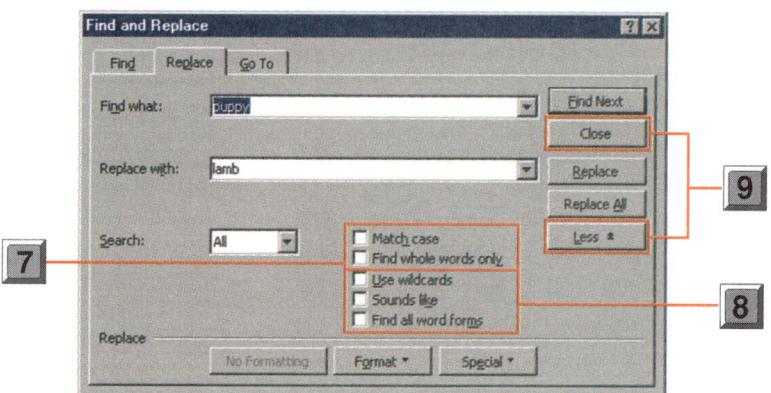

Typing Timesavers

26

❖ **Creating and Using AutoText Entries**

If you use certain blocks of text frequently, you can tell Word to "memorize" them as AutoText entries, which you can then insert into any document with just a few keystrokes. Word makes your AutoText entries available to all future documents you create. In this lesson, you create two AutoText entries, and then you generate a letter by using them as well as one of the AutoText entries that comes with Word.

Creating an AutoText entry

1 Start Word. Or, if you're already in Word, start a new document. Then choose View, Toolbars, AutoText to display the AutoText toolbar. (You can issue all of the AutoText-related commands via the Insert, AutoText menu, but it's simpler to use the AutoText toolbar.)

2 Type the text shown in the figure on the facing page, pressing Enter twice at the end. (AutoText entries can be of any length—from a phrase or two to an entire letter.)

3 Select the text, including the blank lines at the end, and click the New button in the AutoText toolbar. In the Create AutoText dialog box that appears, type **info-request**, and click OK.

4 Press Ctrl+End to move to the end of the document. Type **Sincerely,** press Enter three times, and type **Theresa Jenner**. Then select the four lines of text you just typed (from *Sincerely* to *Jenner*), click the New button in the AutoText toolbar, type the name **closing**, and click OK.

Using an AutoText entry

5 Close the document without saving it (Word has already saved your AutoText entries) and start another document. Press Alt+Shift+D to insert the date and press Enter twice. Now you'll use one of Word's AutoText entries to insert the salutation. Type **To W**. When an AutoComplete tip appears suggesting the AutoText entry *To Whom It May Concern,* press Enter to insert it.

6 Press Enter two more times, and then type **info**. When the AutoComplete tip appears for the *info-request* entry, press Enter. The AutoComplete tip typically pops up after you've typed the first four characters of the AutoText entry's name.

> ℹ You can also insert an AutoText entry you've created by typing the entry's name and then pressing F3 when the insertion point is just past the name. This is the fastest method if the name of the entry is fewer than four characters long.

7 Type **clos**, and when the AutoComplete tip for the *closing* entry appears, press Enter.

8 Save the letter under the name **Groomer Info** in your My Documents folder, and then close the letter and exit from Word.

> ℹ You can also insert AutoText entries by choosing Insert, AutoText, pointing to a category in the list that drops down, and clicking the entry's name. Many of the categories contain entries that come with Word (the *To Whom It May Concern* entry is listed under Salutation, for example). All of the entries you create will be listed under Normal, unless some of your entries are formatted with styles other than the Normal style. (You'll learn about styles in the "Styles" section later in this book.)

Typing Timesavers

26

Quick Reference Bar

AutoText Toolbar

Microsoft Word - Document1
File Edit View Insert Format Tools Table Window Help
Normal
Times New Roman
12
All Entries
New...
I'm collecting information from San Francisco dog groomers such as yourself about your fees and services. Once I've gathered the data, I'll assemble it into a brochure to distribute to pet stores across the city. The brochure should help dog owners find you!
Please fax your information to 415-886-4884 by July 31. If you have any questions, feel free to call me at 415-886-4883.

2

3

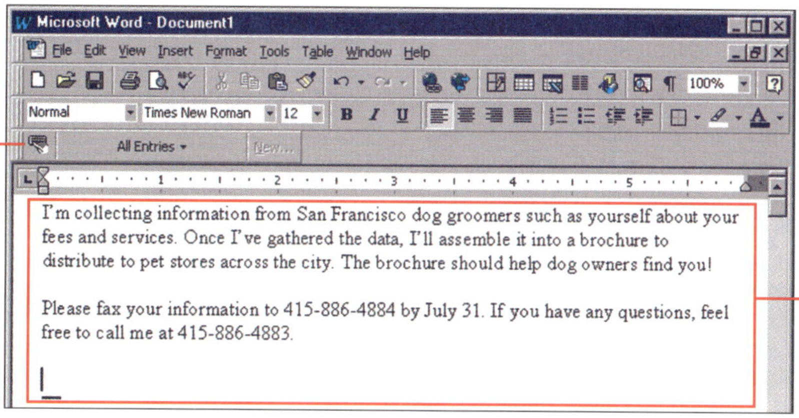

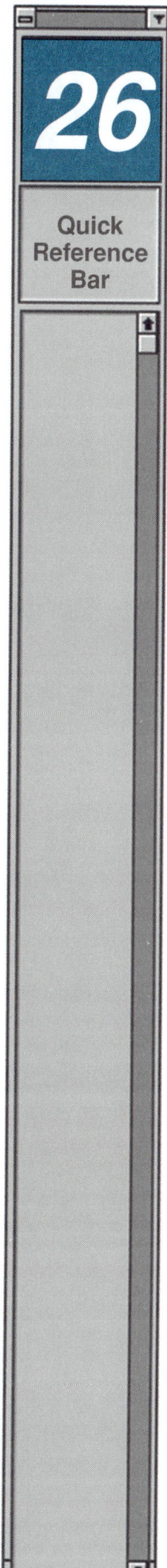

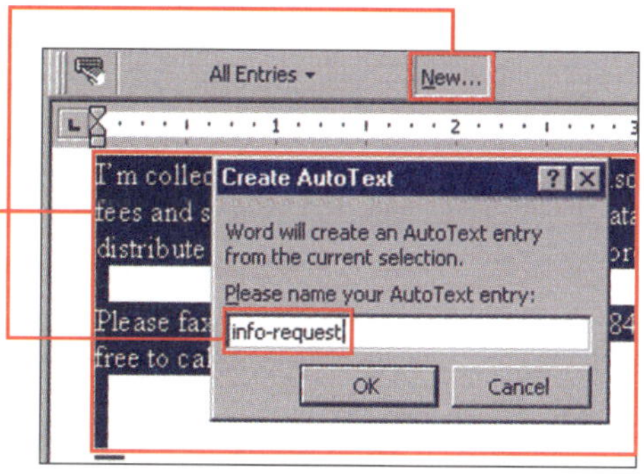

All Entries
New...
Create AutoText
Word will create an AutoText entry from the current selection.
Please name your AutoText entry:
info-request
OK
Cancel

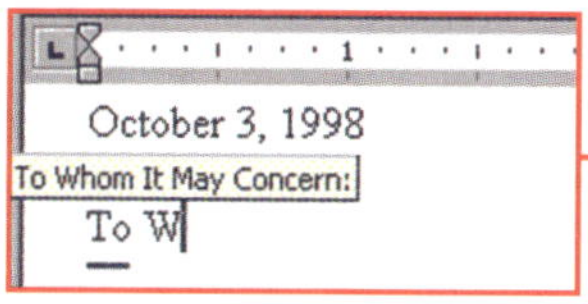

October 3, 1998
To Whom It May Concern:
To W

5

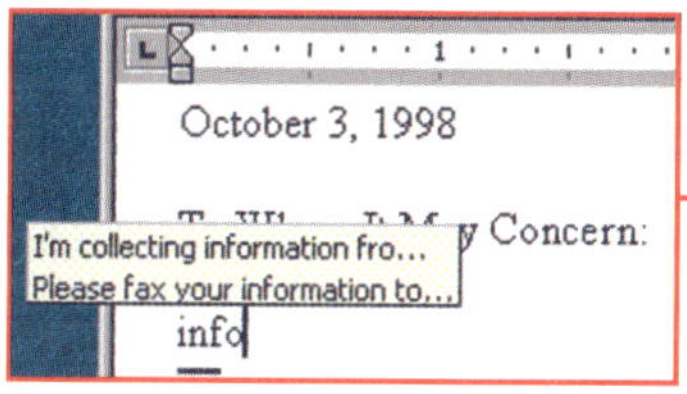

October 3, 1998
I'm collecting information fro...
Please fax your information to...
Concern:
info

6

Please fax your information
free to call me at 415-886-
Sincerely,
Theresa Jenner
clos

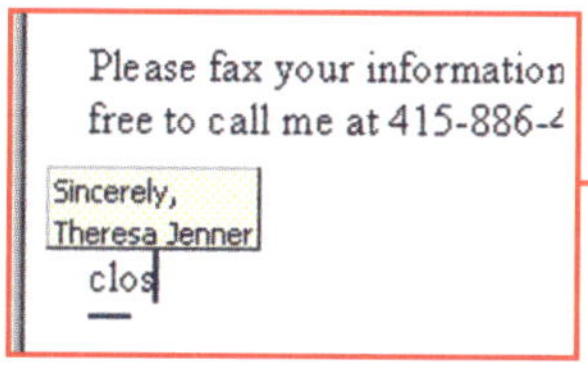

7

Typing Timesavers

27

❖ **Modifying, Deleting, and Printing AutoText Entries**

In this lesson, you modify the content of the AutoText entry named closing that you created in the previous lesson, you delete the info-request entry you created, and you learn how to print a list of entries.

1 Start Word and open the Groomer Info letter from the My Documents folder. If the AutoText toolbar isn't displayed, choose View, Toolbars, AutoText to bring it into view.

Modifying an AutoText entry

2 Change *Sincerely* to *Sincerely yours* in the closing of the letter. Then delete the name *Theresa Jenner* and replace it with your own name. (If an AutoComplete tip for your name appears, just press Enter to insert the rest of your name. This might happen because Word comes with an AutoText entry containing the name of the registered Word user on your computer.)

> ℹ Whenever you want to modify an AutoText entry, you need to start by inserting it into a document (any document will do) so that you can revise its text. In this case, you already had the text of the *closing* entry in the Groomer Info document.

3 Select from *Sincerely* through your last name, and click the New button in the AutoText toolbar. Type the same name you used for this entry before, **closing**, and click OK.

> ℹ When you select an entry you've just revised, make sure to include all of the text you want in the entry, not just the portion you edited.

4 Word asks if you want to redefine the AutoText entry. Click Yes.

> ℹ If you have the Office Assistant displayed (see the earlier lesson "Getting Help with the Office Assistant"), the message box asking if you want to redefine the AutoText entry will look different than the one shown on the facing page.

5 The closing text should still be selected. Press Delete to delete it, type **clos**, and press Enter when the AutoComplete tip appears. This time, Word inserts the revised AutoText entry.

Deleting an AutoText entry

6 Click the AutoText button at the left end of the AutoText toolbar to display the AutoText tab of the AutoCorrect dialog box.

7 In the Enter AutoText Entries Here text box, type **inf** to quickly scroll down the alphabetical list of entries to the ones beginning with the letters *inf*. When you find *info-request*, click it, and click the Delete button. Then click OK.

Printing a list of Auto-Text entries

8 If you want to print a list of AutoText entries, including your own and the ones that came with Word, choose File, Print. Display the Print What drop-down list in the lower-left corner of the Print dialog box, choose AutoText Entries, and click OK. Word prints the list in alphabetical order by name, with the contents of each entry displayed under the name.

9 Save and close the Groomer Info letter, and close Word.

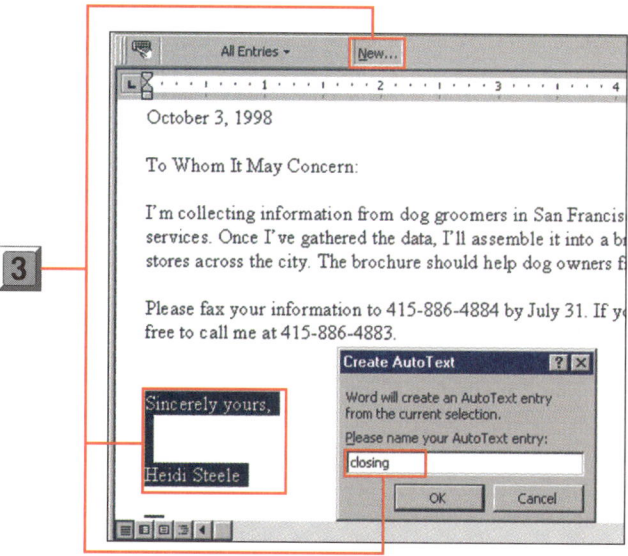

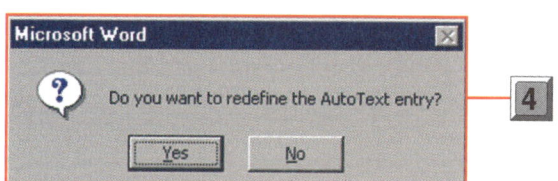

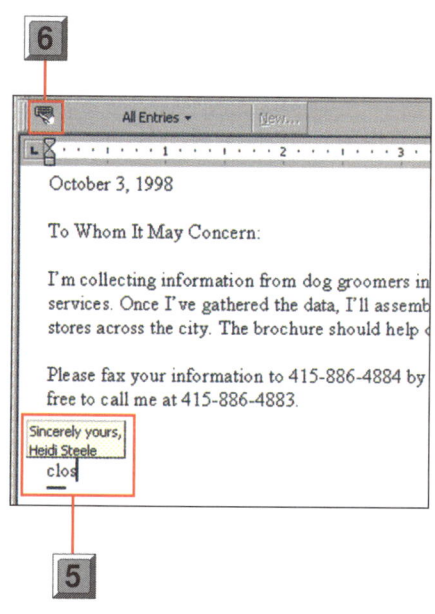

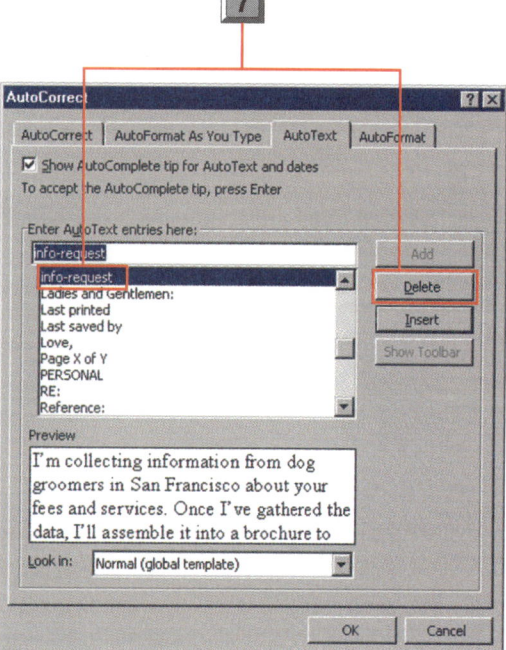

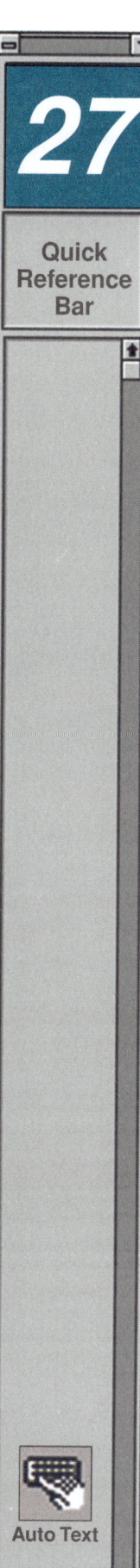

28

Working with Long Documents

❖ **Controlling Page Breaks**

When you type multiple-page documents, Word ends each full page with a soft page break (or automatic page break). These page breaks appear in Normal view as horizontal dotted lines. As you add or delete text, Word adjusts the position of soft page breaks accordingly. Occasionally, you may need to insert a hard page break (or manual page break) to force a page to break before it is full. You could, for example, insert a hard page break to force a new section of a report to begin at the top of the next page.

1 Start Word and open the Reply to Sanders letter. Choose View, Normal to switch to Normal view if you aren't already using this view.

2 Replace the paragraph *In the meantime, here is the price list for our key products:* with **In the meantime, please refer to the attached price list for our key products.** Then press Ctrl+End to move to the end of the letter.

3 Press Ctrl+Enter to insert a hard page break. Hard page breaks are distinguished from soft page breaks by the words *Page Break* in the middle of the dotted line. The insertion point is now below the hard page break. Look at the status bar; it shows that the insertion point is on page two of a two-page document.

4 Select the three lines of the price list and the blank line beneath it. Point to the selection, and drag until the dotted insertion point is just below the hard page break.

5 Release the mouse button to move the selected text onto the second page, and then click once to deselect the text. (See "Moving and Copying Text" earlier in this book if you need more help with drag-and-drop.)

6 Click the Print Preview button in the Standard toolbar to switch to Print Preview. To view both pages of the document, click the Multiple Pages button and drag across two squares in the grid that drops down. Close the Print Preview window. (See "Print Preview" earlier in this book if you need help.)

7 Save and close the document, and then close Word.

ℹ️ To delete a hard page break, click on the page break and press the Delete key.

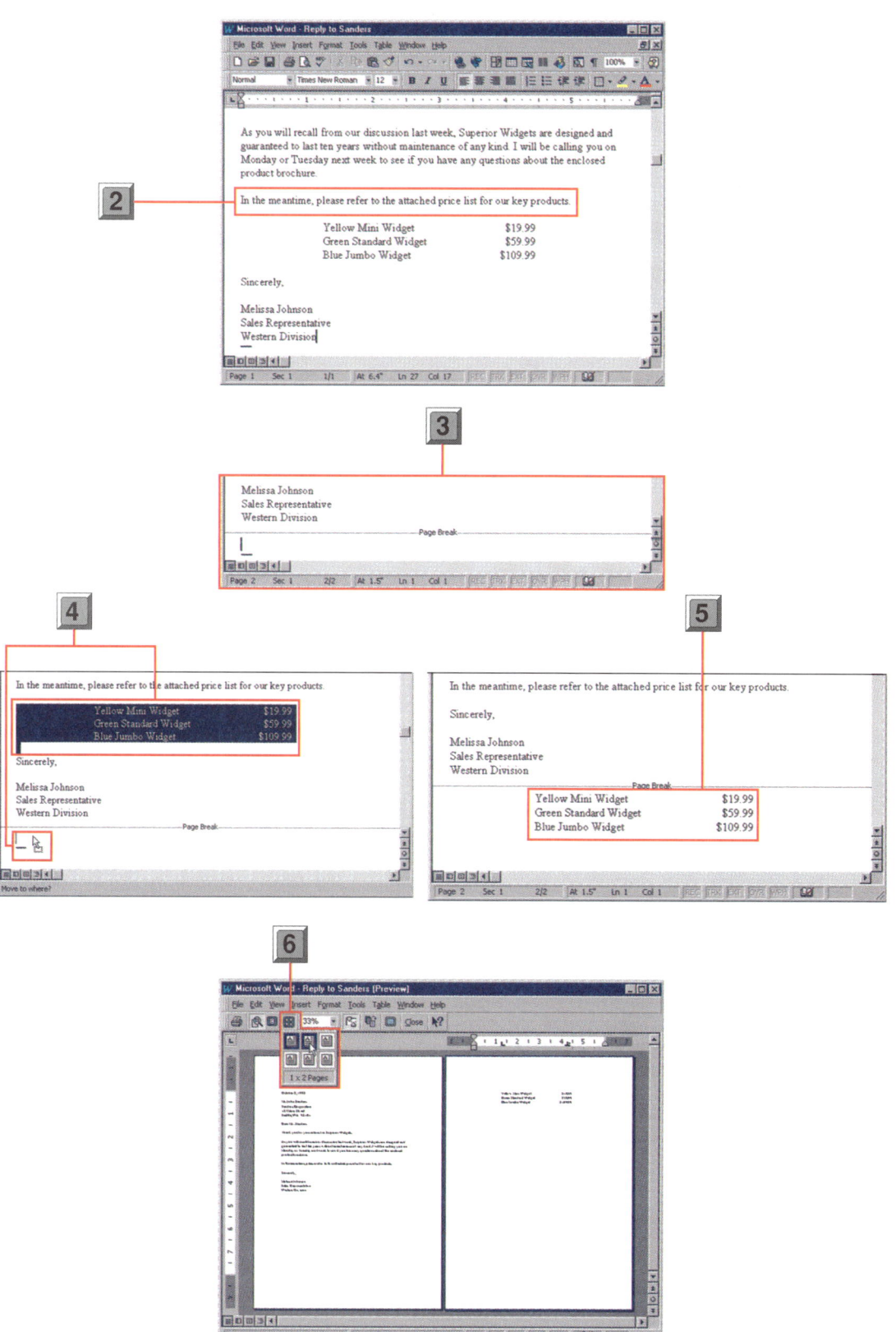

29 Working with Long Documents

❖ **Using Section Breaks**

Section breaks are not particularly glamorous, but they are extremely useful. By default, Word applies page formatting—margins, paper size and orientation, headers and footers, columns, and so on—to all of the pages in your document. If you want to vary the page formatting, you have to divide the document into multiple sections. You can insert as many section breaks in a document as you need to and then apply page formatting in each one independently. This lesson illustrates how to use the two main types of section breaks: continuous and next page.

1 Start Word. If you have a document that's two or more pages long to experiment with, open it now. Otherwise, you can simply review the steps to familiarize yourself with the basic concepts.

Inserting a next page section break

2 The document shown on the facing page is in landscape orientation (see "Changing Margins, Paper Size, and Orientation" earlier in this book). But the second page of the document is a schedule of events, which will look better in portrait orientation. To use different orientation for each page, you need to divide the document into two sections.

3 Click where you want the break to go (just past the word *Valley* in the sample document), and choose Insert, Break to display the Break dialog box. In this example, click the Next Page option button to insert a *next page* section break, which both starts a new section and forces the text beneath the break onto a new page. Click OK.

4 In Normal view, the section break appears as a double line with the words *Section Break (Next Page)* in the middle; when the insertion point is underneath the break, the status bar informs you that you're in section 2.

5 If you leave the insertion point in section 2 and change the orientation to portrait, the change affects only the second page. (The figure on the facing page shows the document in Print Preview.)

Inserting a continuous section break

6 With a document such as the newsletter shown on the facing page, you might want to center the title across the page, but format the text underneath the title in two columns. To do this, you have to insert a *continuous* section break at the beginning of the text you want in columns. This type of break starts a new section but doesn't force the text beneath the break onto the next page.

> ℹ The remaining two types of section breaks, *even page* and *odd page,* are useful if you are creating a long document that you will bind and print on both sides of the paper. They let you specify that the section after the break must begin on the next even page or odd page.

7 This time, choose Insert, Break, click the Continuous option button, and click OK. In Normal view, the break appears as a double line with the words *Section Break (Continuous)* across the middle.

8 You can now apply a two-column format to section 2 (see "Creating and Formatting Columns" later in this book) without affecting section 1, which contains the title. (The document is shown in Page Layout view on the facing page.)

Working with Long Documents

2

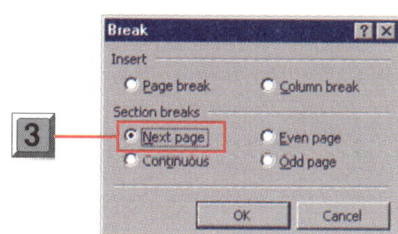

3

4

5

6

8

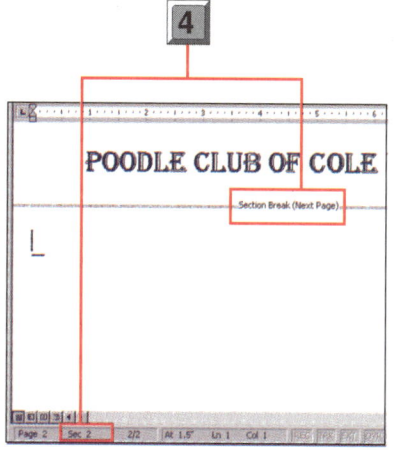

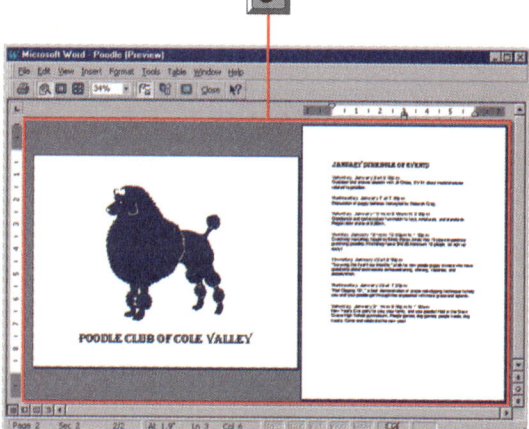

SAVINA Update

CD Release Party, Come Celebrate!

We're having a dance party on April 6 at Ashkenaz to launch the release of our new CD, Echoes from the Mountain. Savina will be singing songs from the CD, and there will be plenty of great Balkan dance music from Golden Thrace and Zapadne Lole, two of the hottest Balkan bands in the Bay Area. Come at 8pm for a dance lesson—performances start at 9pm. Bring your friends!

Zdrastvaytye!
Greetings from the Director

Savina Women's Folk Choir is now in its 16th year (can you believe it?), and we are excited to be producing our first newsletter as a nonprofit arts organization. We anticipate renewing old acquaintances and forging new friendships as we tell you more about who we are and what we're doing.

SAVINA Update

CD Release Party, Come Celebrate!

We're having a dance party on April 6 at Ashkenaz to launch the release of our new CD, Echoes from the Mountain. Savina will be singing songs from the CD, and there will be plenty of great Balkan dance music from Golden Thrace and Zapadne Lole, two of the hottest Balkan bands in the Bay Area. Come at 8pm for a dance lesson—performances start at 9pm. Bring your friends!

Zdrastvaytye!
Greetings from the Director

Concert Schedule

Saturday, April 6 at 8:00 PM
CD release party at Ashkenaz
Savina and two Balkan dance bands
1317 San Pablo Ave. in Berkeley
Tickets: $10
For information: 510-525-5054

Saturday, April 27 at 8:00 PM
Savina and Golden Thrace
Covenant Presbyterian Church
670 E. Meadow in Palo Alto
Tickets: $10
For information: 415-322-9441

30 *Working with Long Documents*

❖ Headers and Footers

A header appears at the top of every page in a document, and a footer appears at the bottom of every page. You can use headers and footers to display the page number, the document title, and so on. You can also place fields in a headers and footers.

1 Start Word, and open the Reply to Sanders letter. Make sure you are in Normal view, and then choose View, Headers and Footers.

2 Word switches to Page Layout view, places the insertion point in the header area, and displays the Header and Footer toolbar, which contains buttons for working with headers and footers. Click the Switch Between Header and Footer button to switch into the footer area.

3 Word creates two custom tabs in the header and footer areas: a center tab in the middle of the page, and a right tab at the right margin. Type your own name at the left margin, and press Tab once to move to the center tab stop.

4 Type **Page**, add a space, and then click the Page Number button on the Header and Footer toolbar to insert the page number. Press Tab again to move to the right tab.

> ℹ️ To delete a field such as the page number or the date, drag across it to select it (the text will be white on a gray background), and then press the Delete key.

5 Click the Date button to insert the current date. This field will update to the current date each time you print.

> ℹ️ If you don't like the format of the date, choose Insert, Date and Time, click the format you'd like to use in the Date and Time dialog box, click the Default button, click Yes, and then click OK. From now on, Word will use the new format when you click the Date button.

6 Select the entire line of text in the footer (click just to the left of the footer area). Then choose 10 from the Font Size list and click the Close button in the Header and Footer toolbar to return to Normal view.

7 Switch to Page Layout view, and scroll to the bottom of each page. The footer is visible in Page Layout view because this view displays the top and bottom margin areas. (To edit a header or footer from here, just double-click on it. Word will activate the header or footer area and display the Header and Footer toolbar.) You can also see headers and footers in Print Preview.

> ℹ️ To omit the header and footer on the first page of your document, choose File, Page Setup, click the Layout tab, mark the Different First Page check box under Headers and Footers, and then click OK. To use different headers and footers in different parts of your document, insert section breaks (see the previous lesson) and then turn off the Same as Previous button in the Header and Footer toolbar in each section.

8 Save and close the document, and then close Word.

Working with Long Documents

Center tab   Right tab

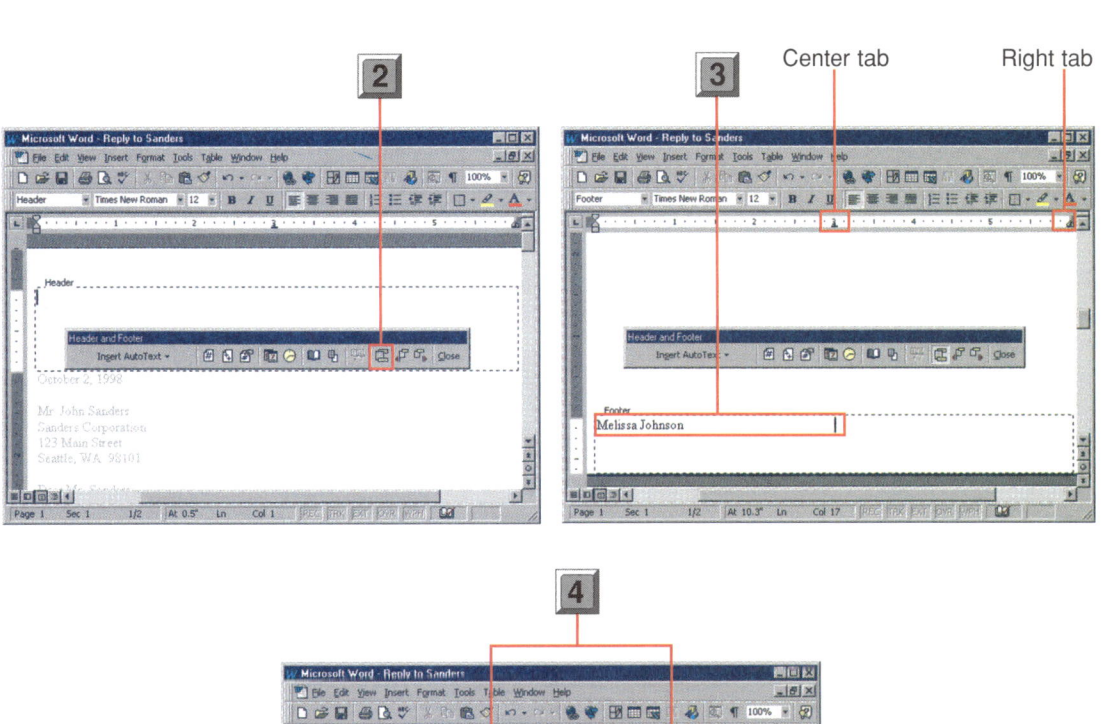

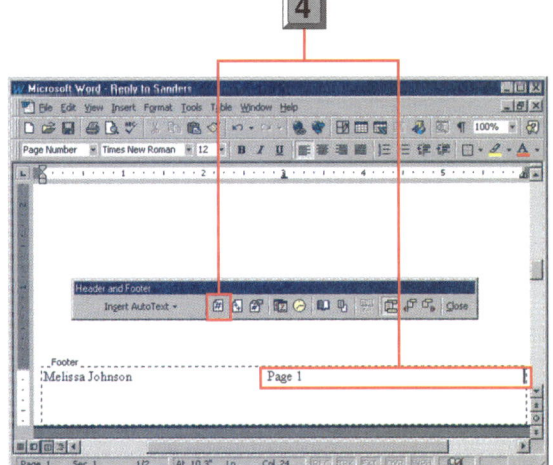

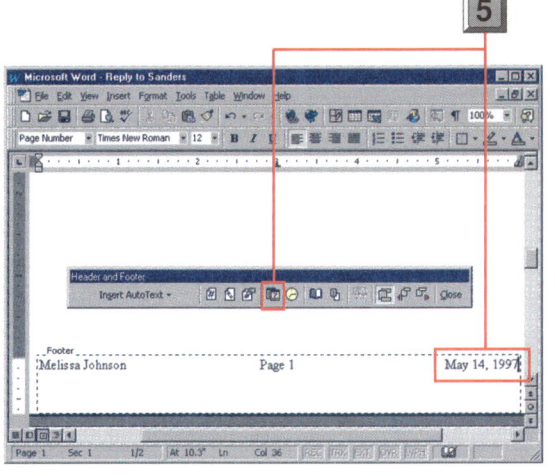

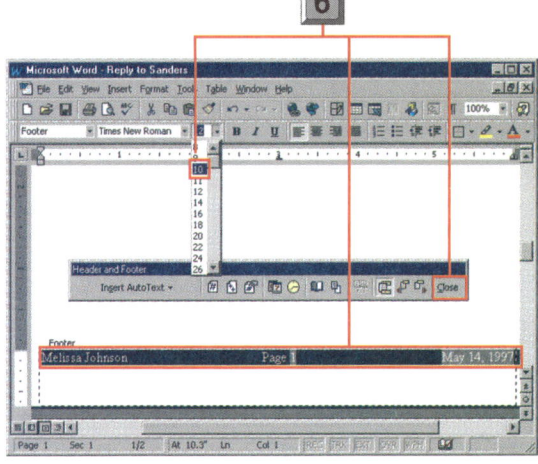

Switch Between Header and Footer

Page Number

Date

Working with Long Documents

31

❖ **Navigating with Browse and Go To**

Browsing is a fast way to move sequentially through a long document—jumping to the next page, heading, footnote, and so on. Go To lets you move nonsequentially to an object of your choosing—skipping directly to a particular page in a long document, for instance.

Navigating with the Browse buttons

1 Start Word and open any long document you have on hand. If your insertion point is not at the beginning of the document, press Ctrl+Home.

2 Point to the Next and Previous buttons in the lower-right corner of the Word window. The default option is to browse by page, so the ToolTips are labeled Next Page and Previous Page. Click the Next button a few times to move from one page to the next. (The left end of the status bar shows what page you're on.) Then click the Previous button a few times to return to the beginning of the document.

3 To browse by a different object, click the Select Browse Object button. Word displays a grid containing various browse objects. Point to each square to see its description at the bottom of the grid, and then click the Heading object. (Browsing by headings only works if you've applied heading styles to your headings; see "Applying Styles" later in this book.)

> ℹ️ The two squares on the left end of the lower row in the Select Browse Object grid—labeled Go To and Find—display the Go To and Find tabs of the Find and Replace dialog box. Go To is described here, and Find is explained in "Using Find and Replace" earlier in this book.

Navigating with Go To

4 As soon as you choose a browse object other than Page, the arrows on the Next and Previous buttons become blue. Point to the Next button; its ToolTip now reads *Next Heading*. Click the Next and Previous buttons to jump from one heading to the next. (Remember, this only works if you've applied heading styles.) Then press Ctrl+Home to go back to the beginning of the document.

5 To use Go To, double-click anywhere along the left two-thirds of the status bar. (You can also choose Edit, Go To, press Ctrl+G, or click the Go To object in the Select Browse Object grid.)

6 Word displays the Find and Replace dialog box with the Go To tab in front. In the Go To What list, select the type of object you want to go to. Choose Page, type a page number in the Enter Page Number box, and click the Go To button. Once you've jumped to the page, click the Close button in the Find and Replace dialog box.

7 Close your document without saving and exit from Word.

> ℹ️ The Find and Replace dialog box is unusual in that it lets you edit your document while the dialog box is on screen. If you see something that needs to be revised while using Go To, just click in the document. The dialog box title bar becomes dim to indicate that the document is active. When you're finished editing the text, click the dialog box title bar to activate it again. Then continue to use Go To, or click the Close button to hide the dialog box.

Working with Long Documents

Previous

Next

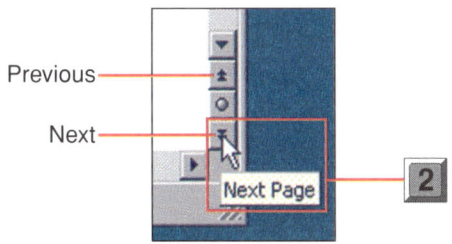

2

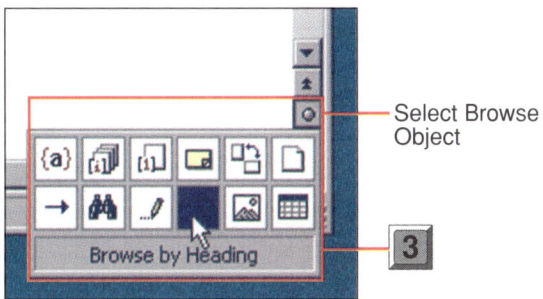

Select Browse Object

3

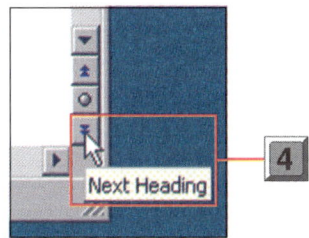

4

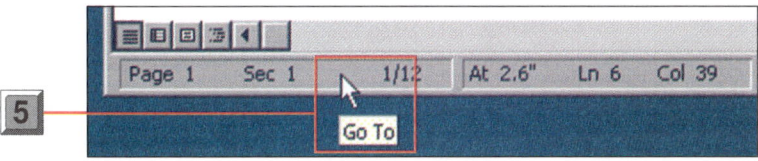

5

6

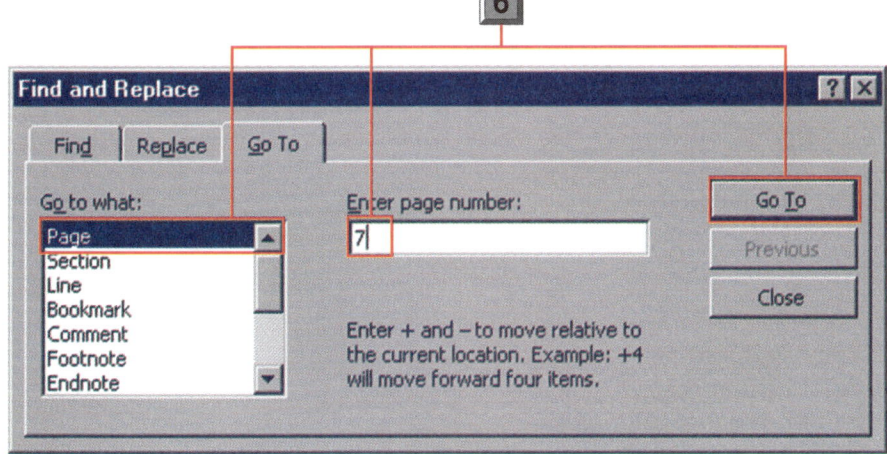

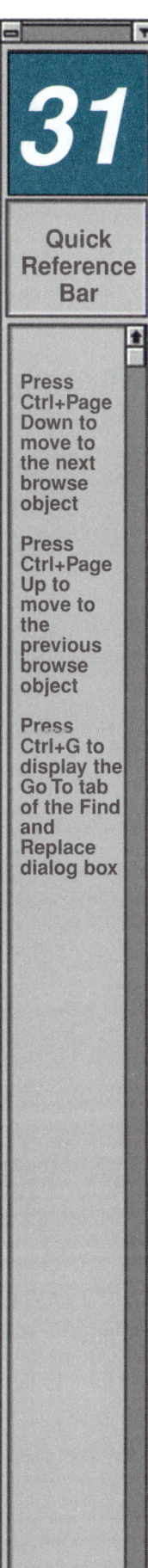

32

Working with Long Documents

❖ **Splitting the Screen**

When you're working with a long document, you may occasionally want to display two parts of the document that are separated by several pages of text. For example, if a report contains a set of figures, you might want to refer to those figures even as you're typing in some other part of the report. You can do this by splitting the screen into two panes and then scrolling each pane independently.

1 Start Word, and open any document you have handy that's more than a page long.

2 Move your mouse pointer over the *split bar,* the short gray horizontal line just above the up scroll arrow at the top of the vertical scroll bar. The mouse pointer changes into two black arrows.

3 Drag down until the gray line representing the split is about halfway down the document window, and then release the mouse button.

> ⓘ You can double-click the split bar instead of dragging it to create a split exactly midway down the window.

4 Your document is now split into two panes. Notice that the window includes separate vertical scroll bars, two rulers, and two sets of Browse buttons. Click in the lower pane to make sure it's active, and use its vertical scroll bar or the down arrow key to move down the document a ways. As you scroll the lower pane, the upper pane stays put. In this example, page 1 of a 10-page document is displayed in the upper pane, and page 10 is displayed in the lower pane. (The status bar shows you the page number for the pane that contains the insertion point.)

> ⓘ When your document is split, you might want to hide the ruler in one or both of the panes so that you have more room to view the text. Click in the pane whose ruler you want to hide, and choose View, Ruler. (Issue this command again when you want to bring the ruler back.)

5 To adjust the position of the split, rest your mouse over the split line. A ToolTip labeled Resize appears and the mouse pointer changes shape. Drag the line up or down, and release the mouse button when the split line is in the right spot.

6 To remove the split, double-click anywhere along the split line.

7 Close the document without saving any changes, and close Word.

> ⓘ You can move or copy text from one pane to the other in a split window. Use any of the techniques for moving and copying text described in "Moving and Copying Text" earlier in this book. And remember, even though you see your document in two separate panes, you are still working with only one document window. So whatever changes you make to the document in one pane are also applied in the other.

Working with Long Documents

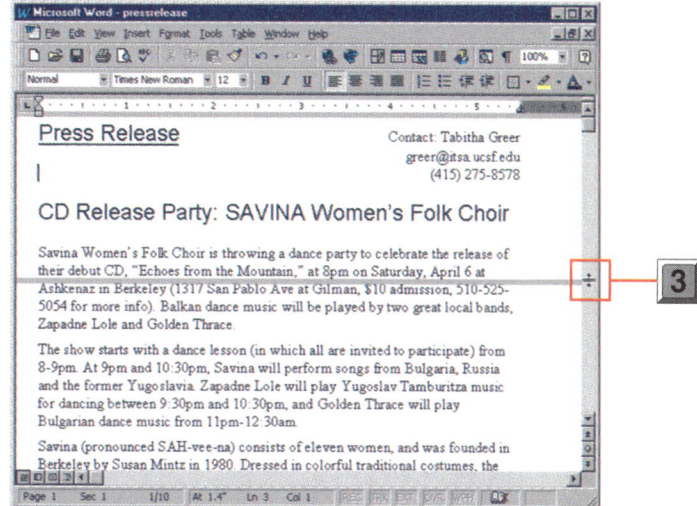

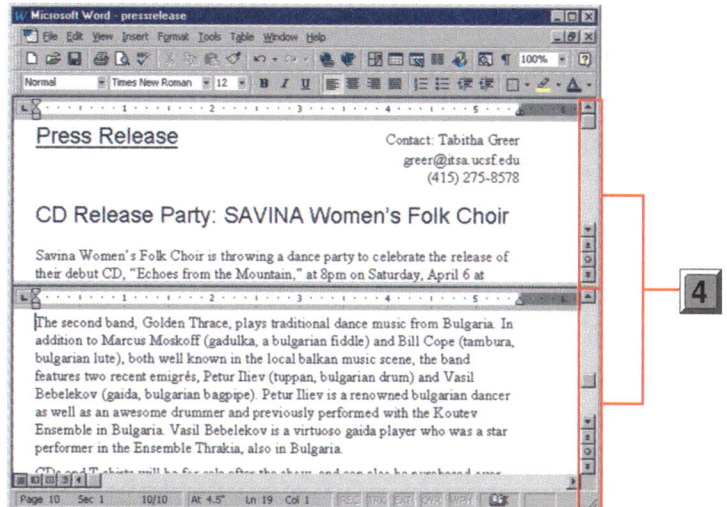

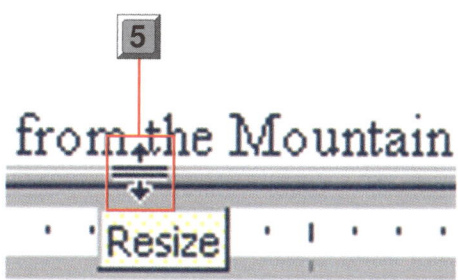

Styles

❖ Applying Styles

A style is a collection of formatting codes to which you've assigned a name. You could, for example, create a style called Section Heading that contains all of the formatting that you use for section headings in reports. Styles let you apply formatting to your documents quickly and consistently. And when you want to change the formatting of a particular element (reduce the size of your section headings, for instance), you don't have to "manually" make the change throughout your document. Instead, you simply revise the style in question, and Word reformats the element for you.

1 Start Word, or start a new document if Word is already open. Then click the down arrow to the right of the Style list box in the Formatting toolbar and click the Heading 1 style.

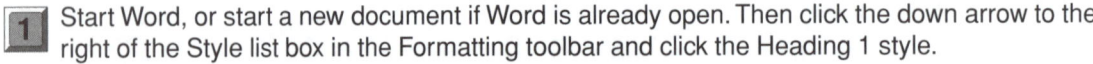

Each template comes with its own set of styles. The blank document that's open now is based on Word's default template, Normal, so the Style list contains the styles that come with this template. (For more on templates, see "Creating a Fax Cover Sheet Using a Template" later in this book.)

2 The Heading 1 style is applied to the paragraph containing your insertion point. (The Style list box now says Heading 1.) If you look at the Formatting toolbar, you can see that the style contains an Arial font, 14-point font size, and boldface. This style also includes some extra spacing above and below the paragraph. (You can change the spacing before and after a paragraph from within the Paragraph dialog box.)

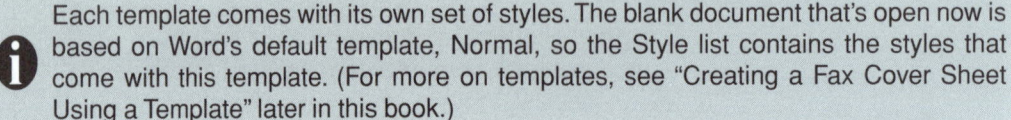

There are two types of styles: character styles and paragraph styles. Character styles can contain only character formatting. In contrast, paragraph styles can contain both character and paragraph formatting, so they are the more flexible of the two. The gray box to the right side of each style in the Style list shows a lowercase *a* for character styles, and a paragraph symbol (¶) for paragraph styles.

3 Type **Tips for Neighbors** and press Enter. Word applies the Normal style to the next paragraph. This is the default style in the Normal template for standard body text. (Word assumes that body text will follow paragraphs formatted with heading styles.) Type the text shown in the figure on the facing page and press Enter. (You can also apply styles by clicking in a paragraph of existing text and then choosing a style from the Style list.)

4 Display the Style list again and this time choose Heading 2. As you can see in the Formatting toolbar, this style includes Arial, 12-point, boldface, and italic. (It also includes some spacing before and after.)

5 Type **Recycling**, press Enter, and continue typing the remainder of the document, applying the Heading 2 style to the Dogs and Noise headings.

6 Click the Tips for Neighbors heading at the top of the document and look at the Style list box. It displays the style you've applied to that paragraph, Heading 1. The quickest way to see what style is in effect for a particular paragraph is to place the insertion point in that paragraph and then look at the Style list box.

7 Save the document in the My Documents folder with the name Neighbors, and then close the document and exit from Word.

Styles

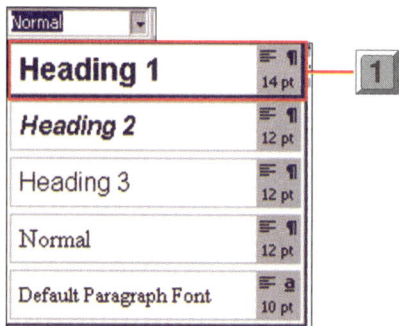

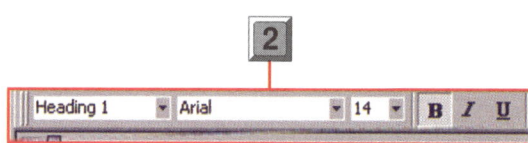

Tips for Neighbors

The neighborhood association is not meeting this summer because experience has shown that attendance is low this time of year. We would, however, like to remind people of a few things, and we look forward to seeing you at our first meeting in September!

Recycling

Pick up on our street is every Tuesday morning. Please put your bins out in the morning and not the night before so that your recycling doesn't get strewn all over the sidewalk.

Dogs

Please clean up after Rover, and keep him on a leash if you have *any* doubts about his friendliness.

Noise

Many of us work at home and/or have young children. If you are planning a party, please let your neighbors know in advance, and be willing to adjust the time/date if necessary.

Styles

❖ **Creating Styles**

When you learned how to apply styles in the previous lesson, you practiced with built-in styles that come with Word. In this lesson, you create your own styles. Word provides several methods for creating styles; the one described here is the most straightforward and flexible. You'll create three styles for the Neighbors document—one for the title, one for the topic names, and one for the body text.

1 Start Word and open the Neighbors document from the My Documents folder. Before you bad break create your own styles, it's a good idea to turn off Word's automatic style feature. When this feature is turned on, Word automatically creates styles based on the formatting you apply. This can get confusing when you're also creating styles of your own. So for now, choose Tools, AutoCorrect, and click the AutoFormat As You Type tab. Clear the check box labeled Define Styles Based on Your Formatting, and click OK. (You can turn the feature back on whenever you like.)

2 Choose Edit, Select All, and choose Normal from the Style list to format all of the paragraphs with the default Normal style. This will make it easier to see the effect of the styles you create. Click once to deselect the text, choose Format, Style to display the Style dialog box, and click the New button.

3 In the New Style dialog box, start by typing **MainTitle** the Name text box.

4 Next, mark the Add to Template check box. If you don't, Word creates the new style but stores it in the document itself, not in the underlying template. If you want the style to be available to other documents, you have to mark this check box.

5 Click the Format button to display a list containing commands that lead to the standard formatting dialog boxes. Start by clicking Font.

6 In the Font dialog box, select a Haettenschweiler 24-point font and mark the Shadow check box. Then click the Character Spacing tab, choose Expanded from the Spacing list, and leave bad break 1 pt in the By text box. (This spreads out the letters a little.) Click the OK button.

7 Click the Format button again, and this time choose Paragraph. In the Paragraph dialog box, type **12 pt** in the Before text box and **3 pt** in the After text box to add some space above and below the title. Click OK to return to the New Style dialog box, and click OK again to return to the Style dialog box.

8 Click the New button again, and this time type the name **Topic** in the Name text box. Repeat steps 4 through 7, but specify a font size of 18 instead of 24.

9 Click the New button one last time, and type the name **Body** in the Name text box. Mark the Add to Template check box, click the Format button, choose Font, and specify a CG Omega 12-pt font (or another font of your choice if this one isn't available). Click OK, click OK again, and then click Close to close the Style dialog box.

10 Click in the first line of the document and display the Style list. Note that the three styles you created appear in the list. Click MainTitle to apply it to the current paragraph.

11 Apply the Topic style to each of the subheadings (Recycling, Dogs, and Noise), and apply the Body style to the paragraphs of body text. The document should look like the one shown on the facing page. Save and close it, and then close Word.

Styles

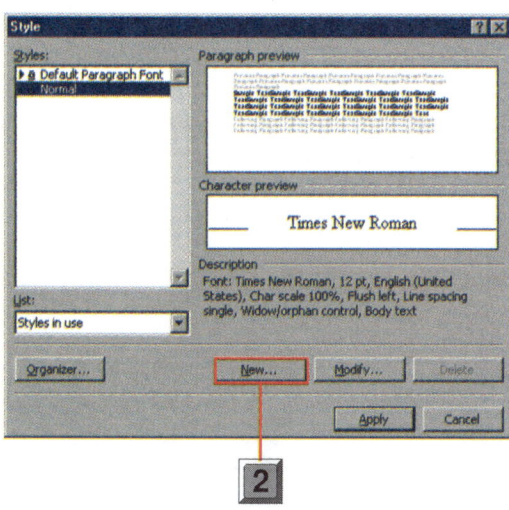

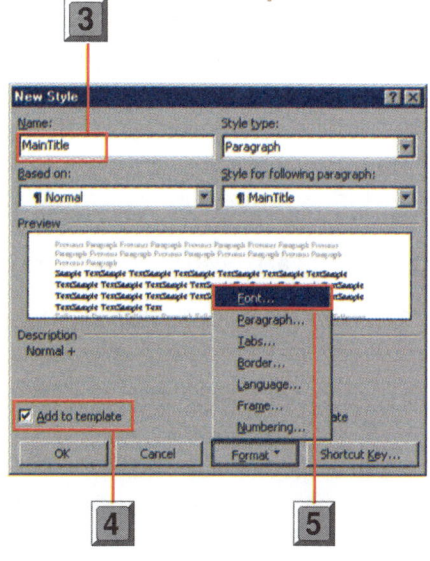

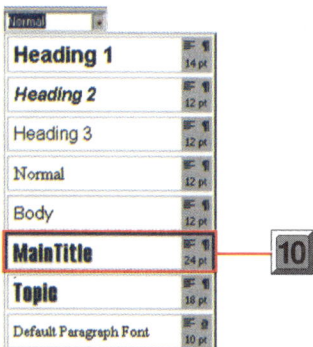

Tips for Neighbors

The neighborhood association is not meeting this summer because experience has shown that attendance is low this time of year. We would, however, like to remind you of a few things, and we look forward to seeing you at our first meeting in September!

Recycling

Pick up on our street is every Tuesday morning. Please put your bins out in the morning and not the night before so that your recycling doesn't get strewn all over the sidewalk.

Dogs

Please clean up after Rover, and keep him on a leash if you have any doubts about his friendliness.

Noise

Many of us work at home and/or have young children. If you are planning a party, please let your neighbors know in advance, and be willing to adjust the time/date if necessary.

Styles

❖ **Modifying Styles**

The beauty of using styles is that if you decide to change the formatting of a particular element of a document, you can just modify the style you applied to that element, and Word will make the change throughout your document in an instant. (Word doesn't apply the change to other existing documents in which you've used the style.) In this lesson, you modify the Body style you created in the previous lesson to add justification and indentation.

1 Start Word and open the Neighbors document from the My Documents folder.

2 Choose Format, Style. Click the Body style in the Styles list on the left side of the Style dialog box, and then click the Modify button.

> **ⓘ** By default, the Styles list in the Style dialog box displays the styles that you have used in the current document. If you like, you can display the List drop-down list in the lower-left corner of the dialog box and choose All Styles to list all of the styles in Word (both the built-in ones and the ones you have created) or User-Defined Styles to list only the styles in the current document that you have created.

3 Notice that the Modify Style dialog box looks just like the New Style dialog box you use to create styles. Mark the Add to Template check box, click the Format button, and choose Paragraph.

> **ⓘ** When you modify a style, you need to click Add to Template if you want the modified version of the style to replace the version stored in the template. If you leave this box cleared, Word stores the modified version of the style in the document, but leaves the original one in the template.

4 In the Paragraph dialog box, choose Justified in the Alignment drop-down list, and type **.2** in the Left and Right text boxes under Indentation to add a slight indent from both the left and right sides. Then click OK to return to the Modify Style dialog box, and click OK again to return to the Style dialog box.

5 All of the formatting in the style, including the formatting you just added, is listed in the Description area. (The New Style and Modify Style dialog boxes have similar Description areas.) Click the Close button.

> **ⓘ** Be careful about using the Apply button in the Style dialog box. You might think that you need to click this button to apply the modified styles to the current document. But you don't; that happens automatically when you click the Close button. The Apply button applies the style that's currently highlighted in the Styles list on the left side of the dialog box to whatever paragraph happens to contain your insertion point.

6 The paragraphs to which you applied the Body style in the previous lesson are now updated with the modified style. (They are now justified and indented from both sides.)

7 Save and close the document, and then exit from Word.

> **ⓘ** To delete a style, choose Format, Style, click the style in the Styles list, and click the Delete button. When Word confirms the deletion, click Yes. When you delete a style, any text to which you've applied the style in the current document reverts to the Normal style, but Word doesn't delete the style from other documents in which you've used it. Word won't let you delete the built-in styles; you can only remove the ones you've created.

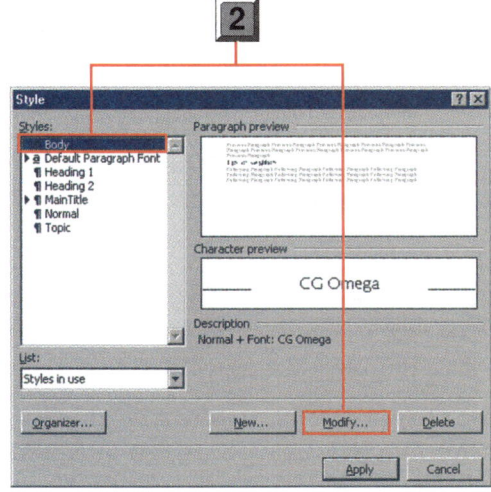

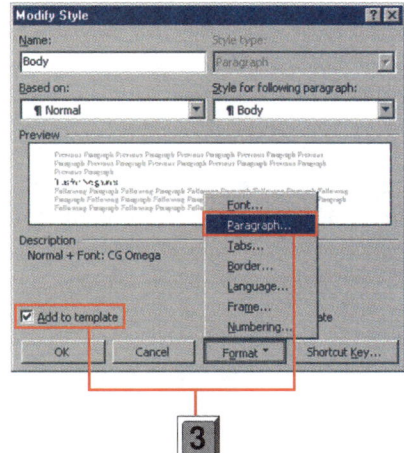

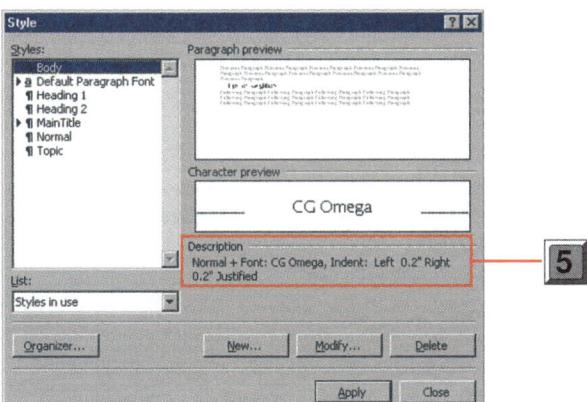

Tips for Neighbors

The neighborhood association is not meeting this summer because experience has shown that attendance is low this time of year. We would, however, like to remind you of a few things, and we look forward to seeing you at our first meeting in September!

Recycling

Pick up on our street is every Tuesday morning. Please put your bins out in the morning and not the night before so that your recycling doesn't get strewn all over the sidewalk.

Dogs

Please clean up after Rover, and keep him on a leash if you have any doubts about his friendliness.

Noise

Many of us work at home and/or have young children. If you are planning a party, please let your neighbors know in advance, and be willing to adjust the time/date if necessary.

36 Templates and Wizards

❖ Creating a Fax Cover Sheet Using a Template

In addition to the default Normal template, Word comes with many other templates designed to help you create specific types of documents quickly. In this lesson, you learn how to use a template to create a fax cover sheet.

1 Start Word, and then choose File, New to display the New dialog box. (Make sure not to click the New button in the Standard toolbar—it doesn't display the New dialog box.)

2 The Normal (Blank Document) template is stored in the General tab of the New dialog box. Click the other tabs to see what additional templates are available. Depending on how Word was installed and whether anyone has created new templates, the tabs and templates you see may differ from the ones shown here.

3 Click the Letters & Faxes tab, and then click the Professional Fax template. When you select a template, Word displays a preview of it on the right side of the dialog box (if a preview is available). Click OK to start a new document based on this template.

4 In a moment, Word displays the document in Page Layout view. If you like, you can increase the magnification of the document by changing the zoom setting. (See "Switching Views and Zooming" earlier in this book if you need help.)

5 Select the words *Company Name Here* in the upper-right corner, and type over them with the name of your company. Then click the text *Click here and type return address and phone and fax numbers*, and type over it with your company's address and phone and fax numbers.

> **ℹ** If you want to use the template in the future and don't want to type your company information every time, you can save this revised version. Choose File, Save As. In the Save As dialog box, display the Save As Type drop-down list, and click Document Template. Optionally, double-click a subfolder of the Templates folder in which you want to store the template. (Each subfolder corresponds to a tab in the New dialog box.) If you save the template in the Template folder itself, it appears in the General tab of the New dialog box. Type a name for the template, and click Save. When you want to use the template in the future, choose File, New, click the appropriate tab, click the template, and click OK.

6 Continue clicking all of the "click here" text and replacing it with your own text. Double-click the Urgent and Please Reply check boxes to mark them. Finally, select the text following *Comments:* and type **We received your proposal today and would like to discuss it with you on Friday morning. Will you be available?**

7 Save the fax cover sheet in the My Documents folder with the name **Practice Fax**. Notice that Word saves it as a Word document, so it doesn't overwrite the template. This lets you reuse the template over and over again.

8 Optionally print the document, close it, and then close Word.

Templates and Wizards

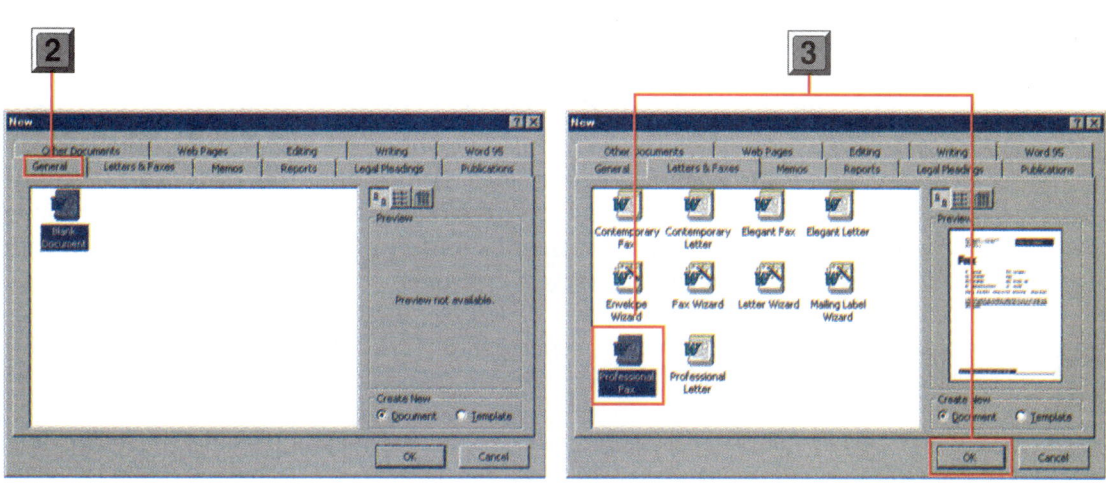

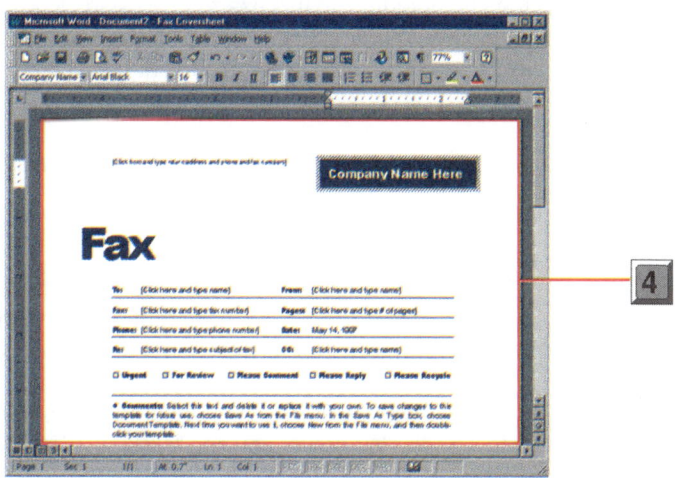

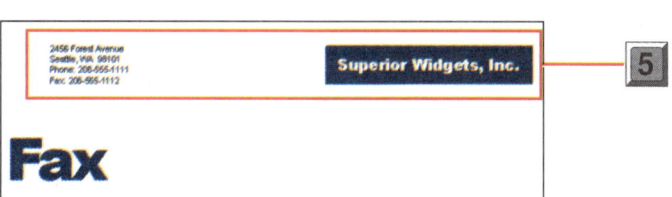

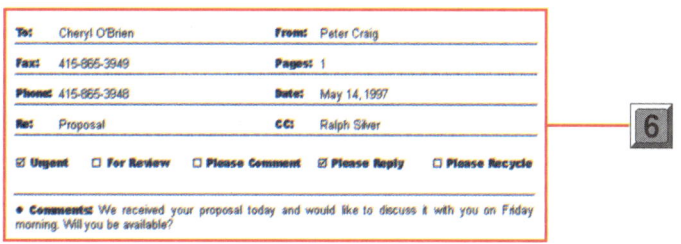

37

Templates and Wizards

❖ **Creating a Memo Using a Wizard**

A Wizard is a specialized template that lets you tailor a template to suit your preferences. Most Wizards ask you questions about what text and formatting you want to include, and then present you with a document that conforms to your requests. Wizard-generated documents look just like documents based on standard templates, complete with "click here" instructions to help you fill in the text. In this lesson, you use a Wizard to help you write a memo.

1 Start Word, and then choose File, New to display the New dialog box. Click the Memos tab, click the Memo Wizard template, and click OK.

2 Word displays the first step of the Wizard, called Start. As you progress through the Wizard, Word highlights the current step on the left side of the dialog box. Click the Next button to move to the next step.

3 The Wizard presents the first question. In this example, it needs to know which style you want to use for your memo. Choose Contemporary, and click Next again. Continue working your way through the steps. If you want to go back to a previous step, click the Back button one or more times.

4 When you reach the Finish step, click the Finish button to tell the Wizard to start generating the document.

5 In a moment, Word displays a document in Page Layout view with the text and formatting you requested, and the Office Assistant appears to ask if you need more help with the memo. For this exercise, click Cancel to close the Office Assistant. (See "Getting Help with the Office Assistant" earlier in this book for more information about this handy tool.)

6 Change the zoom setting if you need to enlarge the document on screen. (See "Switching Views and Zooming" earlier in this book.) Wherever you see "click here" instructions, replace them with actual text.

7 Print the document if you like, and then close it without saving, and close Word.

Templates and Wizards

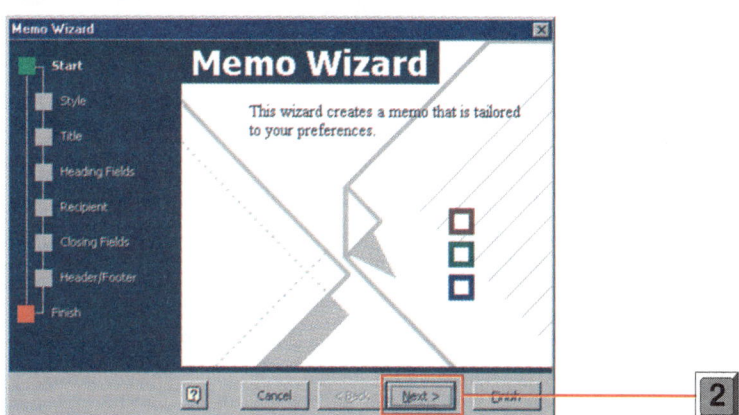

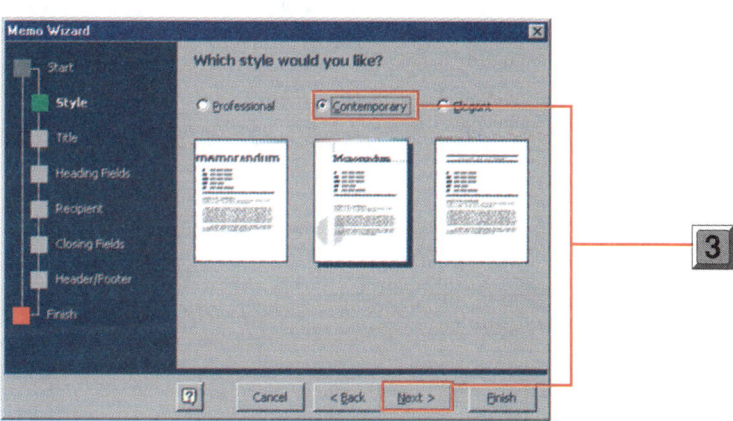

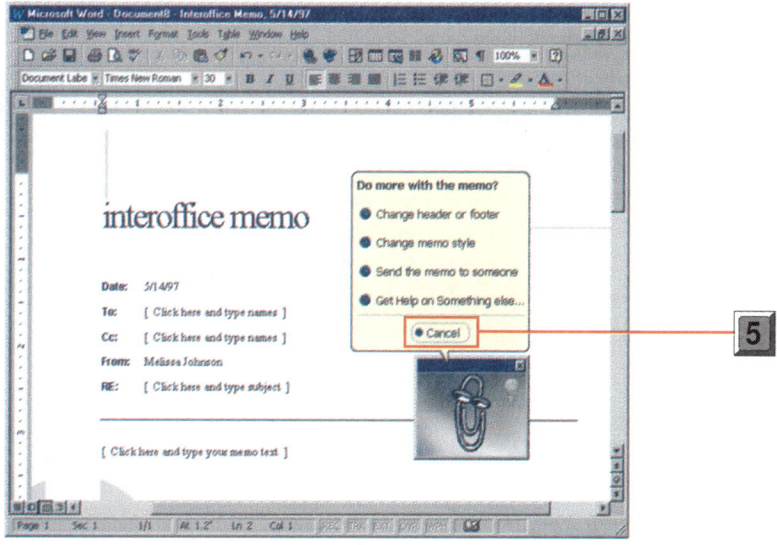

38 Columns and Tables

❖ **Creating and Formatting Columns**

If you want to create newspaper-style columns—that is, columns in which text flows down one column and then snakes up to the top of the next—you need to use Word's column feature. You can revise a document after you've applied columns, but it's usually easier to edit your text first, and then apply columns as a last step before printing. As with other page formatting features, columns affect the entire document unless you divide it into sections.

1 Start Word, and then open any document that's at least one page long to practice with.

2 Switch to Page Layout view (View, Page Layout). Word can't display columns in Normal view, so it's easiest if you switch to Page Layout view before creating them.

> ℹ️ If you don't want columns in the entire document, insert section breaks where necessary to separate the text to which you want to apply columns into its own section. See "Using Section Breaks" earlier in this book if you need a refresher on section breaks.

3 Click the Columns button in the Standard toolbar. A grid drops down containing vertical bars representing columns. Point to the third bar, and click once.

4 Word formats your text in three columns. Try pressing Alt+Down Arrow to move column by column to the right, and Alt+Up Arrow to move column by column to the left.

5 Click the Columns button again and click the second bar in the grid to change to two columns. (To remove multiple columns, just click the leftmost bar in the grid.)

> ℹ️ If you need to force text from the bottom of one column to the top of the next, position the insertion point where you want to break the text and press Ctrl+Shift+Enter to insert a column break.

6 Choose Format, Columns to display the Columns dialog box. Mark the Line Between check box to add a vertical line between your columns and click OK.

> ℹ️ The top of the Columns dialog box contains some preset formats for multiple columns of varying numbers and widths. If you have specific requirements for the width of each column and the amount of space between columns, clear the Equal Column Width check box, and then enter the desired settings for each column under Width and Spacing.

7 Word adds a line between the two columns. Now select the entire document, click the Justify toolbar button to apply justified paragraph alignment, and then click once to deselect the text.

> ℹ️ You can reduce the obvious gaps between words in justified column text by turning on hyphenation for the document. Choose Tools, Language, Hyphenation, mark the Automatically Hyphenate Document check box, and click OK.

8 Close the document without saving, and then exit from Word.

> ℹ️ The last page of a multiple-column document can look awkward if there is not enough text to fill all the columns. To balance the columns on the last page, insert a continuous section break at the end of the last column.

Columns and Tables

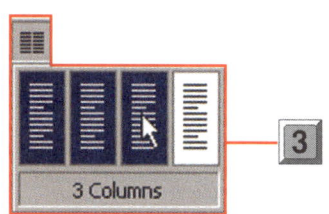

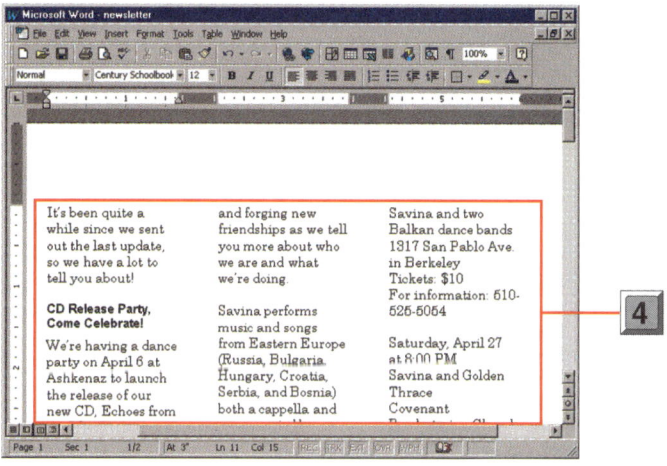

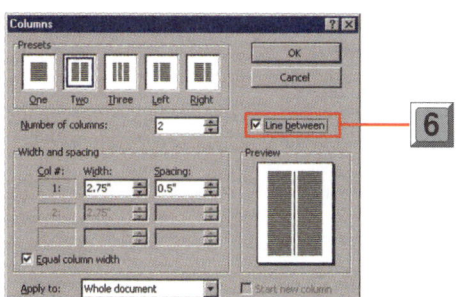

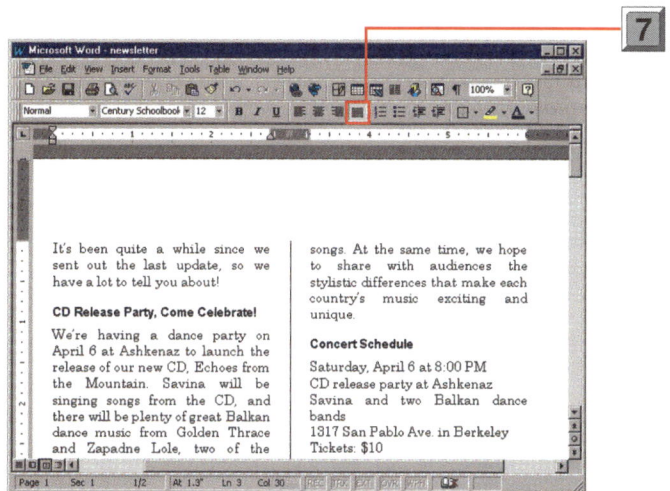

38

Quick Reference Bar

Press Alt+Down Arrow to move to top of next column

Press Alt+Up Arrow to move to top of previous column

Press Ctrl+ Shift+ Enter to insert a column break

Columns

Columns and Tables

39

❖ **Creating a Table**

A table is a grid you use to line up text in rows and columns. You type text into the individual boxes (called cells) in the table, and you have complete control over the appearance of the borders—from no borders to ornate three-dimensional ones. Tables are great for creating anything from simple charts to invoices or employee lists.

1 Start Word, or if Word is already open, start a new document.

2 If you aren't in Page Layout view, switch to it now (View, Page Layout). Type **Food for Memorial Day Weekend Backpacking Trip**, press Enter twice, and then click the Tables and Borders button on the Standard toolbar.

3 Word displays the Tables and Borders toolbar. (It might be floating or docked on one side of the Word window. To find out how to move a toolbar, ask the Office Assistant to search for help topics related to *moving a toolbar*—see the earlier lesson "Getting Help with the Office Assistant.") Click the Draw Table button if it isn't already pushed in. The mouse pointer becomes a small pencil. Choose View, Ruler if the vertical and horizontal rulers aren't displayed. Starting two lines beneath the text, drag diagonally down to the 2.5-inch mark and to the right to the 5-inch mark, and then release the mouse button.

> ℹ️ If you want to create a large table, it's faster to use the Insert Table command than to draw the table with the mouse. Choose Table, Insert Table, type the number of rows and columns you want, and click OK.

4 Drag with the mouse to draw three vertical and three horizontal lines approximately evenly spaced across the table. As you drag, a dashed line shows you where the line will be inserted. Release the mouse button as soon as the line extends across the entire width or height of the table. Don't worry if the rows and columns aren't even. You'll fix them in the upcoming lesson "Formatting a Table."

> ℹ️ If you insert a table at the very top of a document and later decide you want to type text above the table, click at the beginning of the upper-left cell in the table and press Enter. Word inserts a blank line above the table and places your insertion point in it to let you start typing.

5 Click the Draw Table button to turn it off, and then enter the text shown on the facing page. When an entry is too wide to fit in a column, Word automatically wraps the text to the next line and increases the row height if necessary to accommodate the text.

> ℹ️ To move the insertion point to a cell, just click in it. You can also move from cell to cell by pressing the four arrow keys, although if a cell contains text, the right and left arrow keys move the insertion point character by character within the cell. Lastly, you can press Tab to move cell by cell to the right, and Shift+Tab to move to the left.

6 Save the document in the My Documents folder with the name Food Planning, and exit from Word.

> ℹ️ To start a new line in a cell, press Enter. To insert a tab in a cell, press Ctrl+Tab (pressing the Tab key by itself moves the insertion point from cell to cell).

Columns and Tables

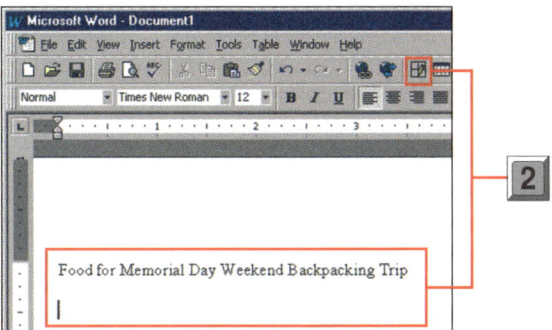

2

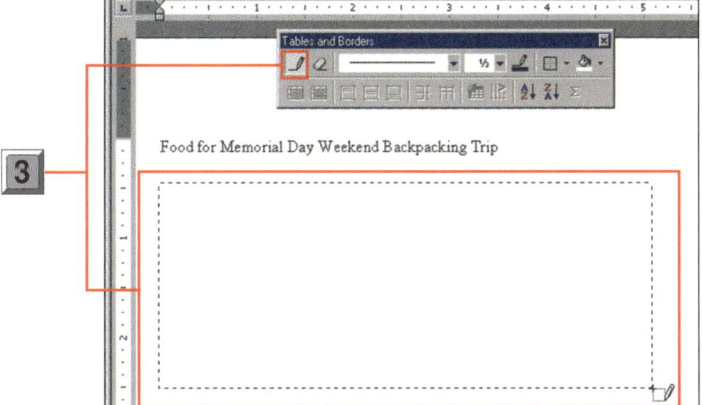

3

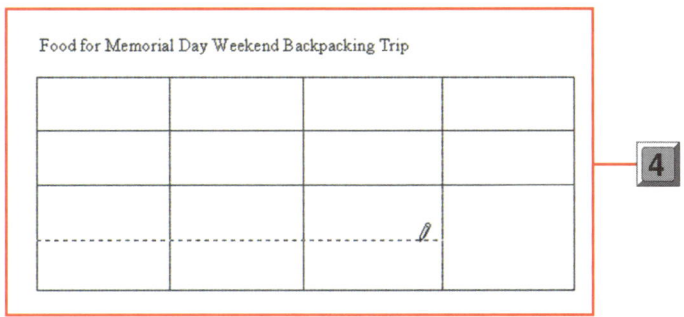

4

Food for Memorial Day Weekend Backpacking Trip

5

	Saturday	Sunday	Monday
Breakfast	Fruit and cold cereal	Oatmeal and raisins	Granola
Lunch	Peanut butter sandwiches	Cheese and crackers	Sardines and crackers
Dinner	Macaroni and cheese	Thai curry stew	

Tables and Borders

Draw Table

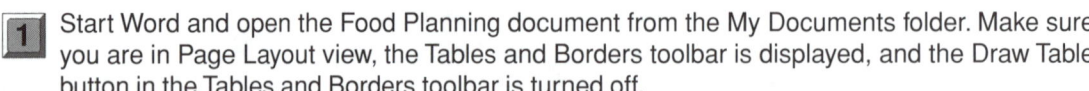

Columns and Tables

❖ **Modifying the Structure of a Table**

As you enter text into a table, you will almost certainly need to change the table's structure. You might need to add or delete a row or column, merge some cells together, or split a cell into smaller cells.

1 Start Word and open the Food Planning document from the My Documents folder. Make sure you are in Page Layout view, the Tables and Borders toolbar is displayed, and the Draw Table button in the Tables and Borders toolbar is turned off.

Inserting a column

2 Point to the top border of the Saturday column. When the mouse pointer changes to a small black arrow, click to select the column. (You can also select a column by holding down the Alt key as you click within the column.) Then click the Insert Columns button in the Standard toolbar to add a column to the left of the selected one. When a column is selected, the Insert Columns button replaces the Insert Table (or Insert Rows) button.

3 Click once to deselect the new column, and then type the text shown on the facing page.

> ℹ️ If you want to add a column at the right end of the table, select the *end-of-row markers* outside the right edge of the table. (You select them just as you would a column. To display the markers, which look like small circles, click the Show/Hide button on the right end of the Standard toolbar.)

Inserting a row

4 Click to the left of the Breakfast row to select it (or just click in the row), and then click the Insert Rows button in the Standard toolbar. When your insertion point is in a table and you don't have a column selected, this button replaces the Insert Table button. (If you want to insert a row at the very bottom of a table, just click in the lower-right cell of the table and press the Tab key.)

> ℹ️ To delete a row or column, select it and then choose Table, Delete Rows or Delete Columns. To delete an entire table, make sure your insertion point is in the table, choose Table, Select Table, and then choose Table, Delete Rows.

Merging cells

5 Click once to deselect the new row, and then click the Eraser button in the Tables and Borders toolbar. With the eraser pointer, drag over the vertical borders between the days of the week in the new row, releasing the mouse button as soon as each border becomes covered with a thick line. (Don't erase the right border of the leftmost column.) Erasing borders merges cells into one larger cell. If you want to keep two cells intact but just hide the border between them, change the line style to No Border (see the next lesson).

> ℹ️ You may at times want to split one cell into two or more cells. To do this, use the Draw Table tool to draw the vertical or horizontal border(s) dividing the cell.

6 Click the Eraser button again to turn it off. Type **Snacks** in the small cell on the left end of the new row and **Dried fruit, trail mix, chocolate bars, lemon drops** in the large cell on the right.

7 Save and close the Food Planning document, and then exit from Word.

Columns and Tables

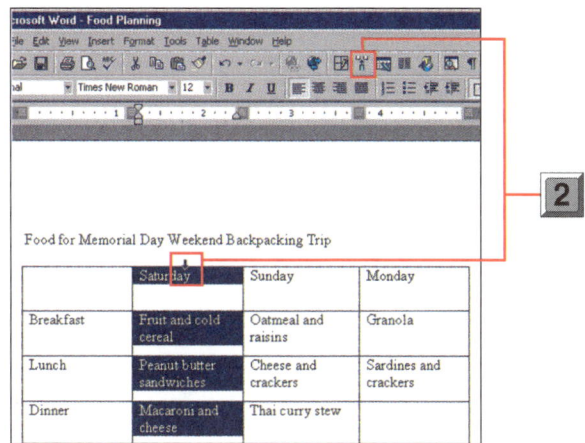

2

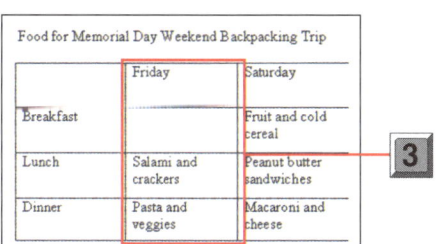

3

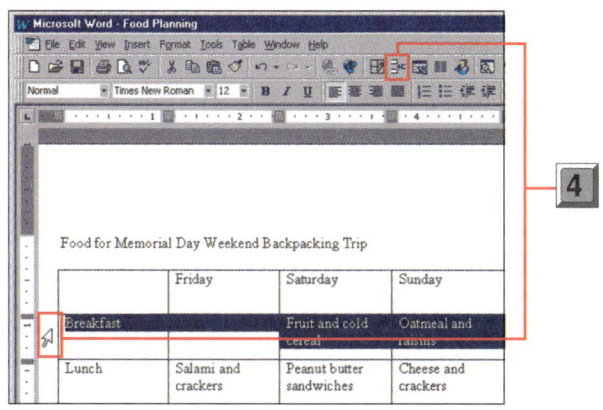

4

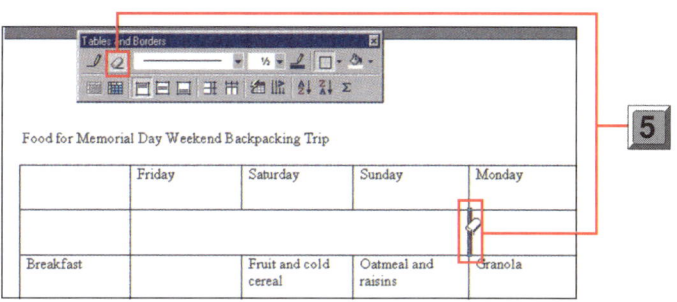

5

Insert
Columns

Insert
Rows

Eraser

Columns and Tables

❖ **Formatting a Table**

Word offers a myriad of ways to format a table and the text it contains. In this lesson, you tinker with the Food Planning table to improve its appearance.

1 Start Word and open the Food Planning document from the My Documents folder. Make sure you are in Page Layout view and the Tables and Borders toolbar is displayed.

2 Make sure your insertion point is in the table, choose Table, Select Table to select the entire table, and click the Center Vertically button in the Tables and Borders toolbar to align the text vertically within each cell.

3 Drag across the four labels in the top row to select them, and click the Bold and Center buttons in the Formatting toolbar. Then select the four labels in the leftmost column and click the Bold button.

4 Hold down the Alt key as you click in the leftmost column to select it, click the down arrow to the right of the Shading Color button in the Tables and Borders toolbar to display a palette of colors, and click the fourth one in the top row (Gray–10%). Now select the top row and apply the same gray shading to it. Then click to deselect the row.

5 Select the Draw Table button in the Tables and Borders toolbar, select the double line option for the Line Style, ∫ for the Line Weight, and confirm that Border Color is set to Automatic. (The Border Color button doesn't have a down arrow next to it, but clicking the button displays a palette of options.) Then drag across the bottom border of the first row. When it is selected (covered with a thick line), release the mouse button to apply the border options you've chosen. Then drag down the right border of the leftmost column to apply the same formatting to this border.

6 Turn off the Draw Table button. Drag the right border of the leftmost column to the left to narrow the column a little, and then drag the bottom border of the top row up to slightly decrease the height of the row.

> ℹ️ Word doesn't prevent you from creating a table that's too wide to fit on the page, so if you are changing column widths or inserting columns, you should check Print Preview frequently. If you want to create a wide table, you might consider switching to landscape orientation. (See "Changing Margins, Paper Size, and Orientation" earlier in this book.)

7 Point to the top border of the Friday column. When you see a small black arrow, drag across to the Monday column to select all columns but the first. Then click the Distribute Columns Evenly button to make these four columns the same width.

8 Starting with the mouse pointer to the left of the Snacks row, drag down to the Dinner row to select all rows but the first, and click the Distribute Rows Evenly button to make these four rows the same height.

> ℹ️ If you want to center your table horizontally on the page, choose Table, Cell Height and Width, click the Row tab if necessary, click the Center option button, and click OK.

9 Save and close the document, and then exit from Word.

Columns and Tables

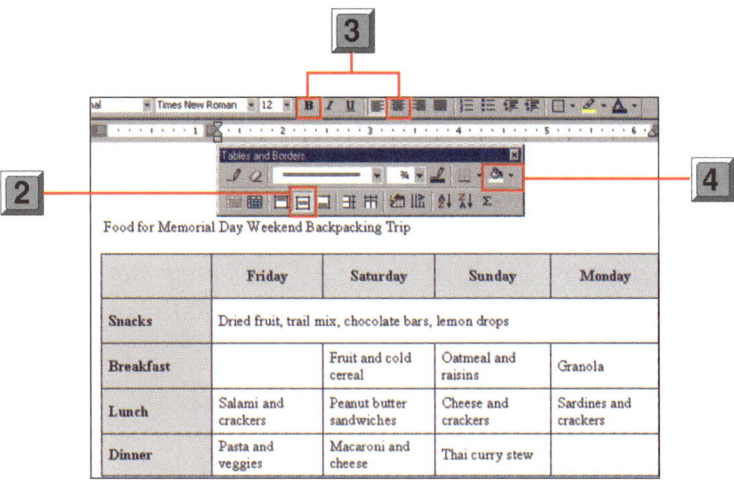

Line Weight

Line Style   Border Color

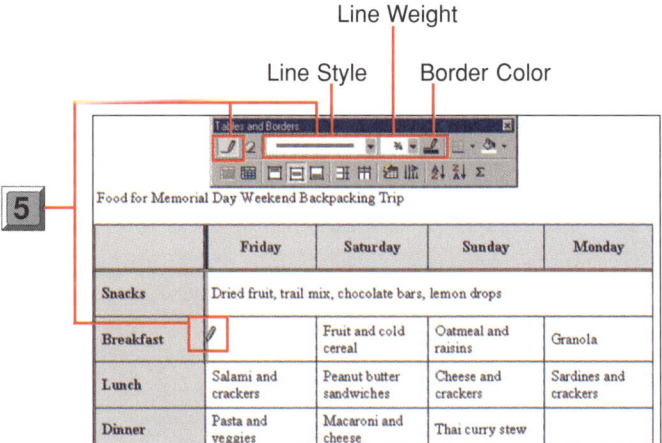

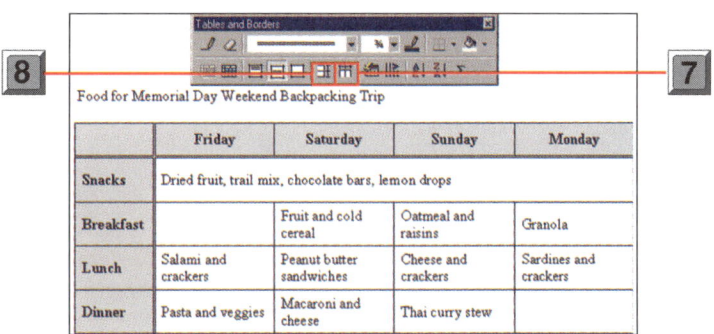

Center Vertically

Shading Color

Border Color

Distribute Columns Evenly

Distribute Rows Evenly

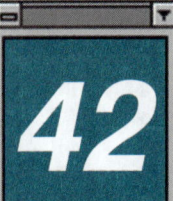

Mail Merge

❖ **Starting the Main Document**

Word's mail merge feature automates the process of inserting personal information such as names and addresses into a document that you want to send to many people. To set up a mail merge, you need to create two documents. The main document is the document you will print, such as a form letter, label, or envelope. The data source is the list of information, usually names and addresses, that Word plugs into the main document. In this lesson, you begin the mail merge process, specifying which document you want to use as your main document. It's best work through this lesson and the next three in one sitting, so make sure you have plenty of time before you start.

1 Start Word. If Word is already open, start a new document and close any other open documents.

2 Save the new blank document in the My Documents folder with the name **Practice-Main**. Then choose Tools, Mail Merge to display the Mail Merge Helper dialog box. (Make sure not to choose Tools, Merge Documents. Despite its name, this command has nothing to do with the mail merge feature.)

> ℹ The Mail Merge Helper guides you through the process of setting up and running the merge. You can initiate all of the steps in a merge from this dialog box, although it's sometimes faster to use toolbar shortcuts.

3 Under Main Document, click the Create button. Word displays a list of the different types of main documents you can create. Click Form Letters.

4 Word asks what document you want to use as your main document. Since you've already started your main document, click the Active Window button.

5 Word displays the name and location of the main document under Main Document and activates the Get Data button. Click the button and choose Create Data Source.

> ℹ If you have an existing data source, choose Open Data Source, select the file from the Open Data Source dialog box, and click the Open button. (If you want to use a list that's stored in a database program such as Access or FoxPro, choose the appropriate file format from the Files of Type drop-down list and then select the file.) Click the Edit Main Document button when prompted, and skip to "Completing the Main Document."

6 The Create Data Source dialog box is where you define which fields (categories of information) you want to use in your data source. Word displays a list of the most typical fields under Field Names in Header Row. In the next lesson, you learn how to remove fields you don't need, add new fields, and change the order of the fields.

7 Go on to the next lesson without closing the document.

> ℹ If you want to use an existing document as your main document, you can open it, remove all of the personal information—such as the name, address, and salutation—and save the document under a new name. When you complete the main document (see the upcoming lesson "Completing the Main Document"), you replace the personal information with merge codes—special codes telling Word to pull the names and addresses from the data source.

Mail Merge

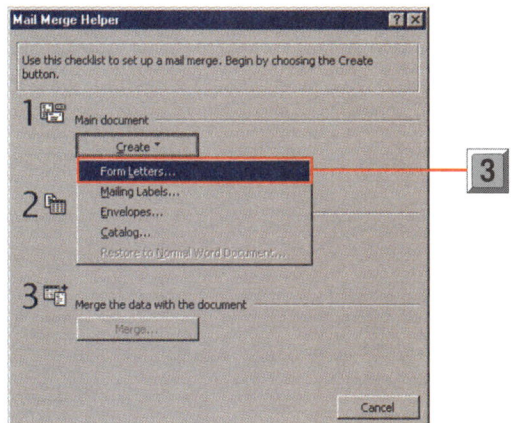

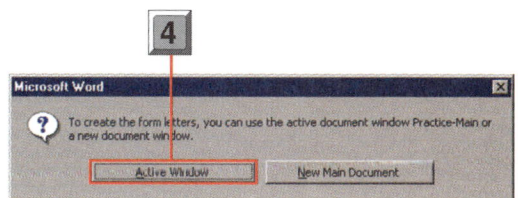

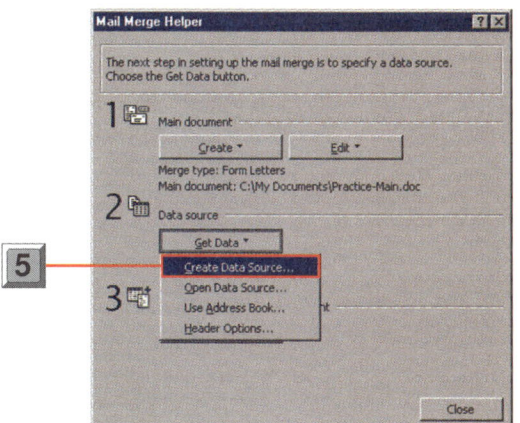

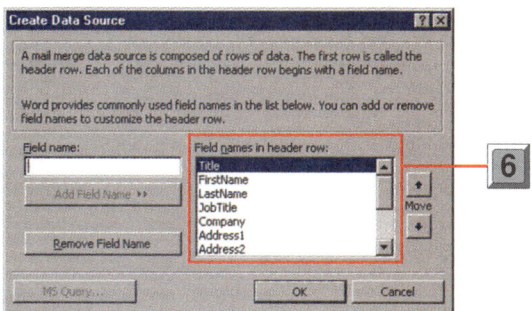

Mail Merge

43

❖ **Creating the Data Source**

Because a data source is a simple database, you need to understand two database-related terms to work with it: record and field. A record is all of the information about one person in your data source. A field is one category of information within each record. In this lesson, you define which fields you want to use, and then you enter the data.

1 The Create Data Source dialog box should still be open from the previous lesson. Click the Title field (if it isn't already selected) on the right side of the dialog box, and click the Remove Field Name button. Then repeat this process to remove the Job Title, Address 2, Country, HomePhone, and WorkPhone fields. You should have seven fields remaining in the list.

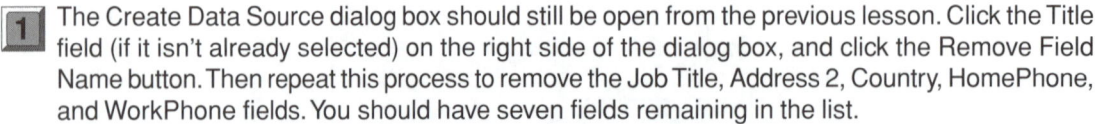

> ⓘ To change the position of a field in the list, click the field and then click the Move arrows. You will be able to place your fields anywhere you like in the main document, in any order. Ordering them in a way that makes sense to you in this dialog box is just a convenience that will make it easier to enter data in your data source.

2 The last field you deleted, WorkPhone, is still highlighted in the Field Name text box. Type over it with **Salutation**, and click the Add Field Name button to add this field to the list on the right. Then click OK.

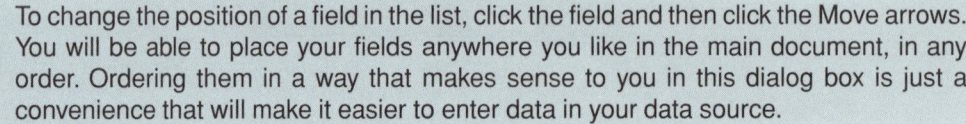

> ⓘ The Salutation field lets you use a name other than the first name or last name after *Dear* in the salutation of a form letter. If a person in your mailing list is named Elizabeth Foutz, for example, and you want to address her letter to *Beth* or *Ms. Foutz*, you would enter one of these options in the Salutation field. (Don't include the word *Dear* in the field; you will type it in the main document itself.)

3 Word displays the Save As dialog box because it needs to save the data source before you enter records. Save the file in the My Documents folder with the name **Practice-Data Source**. Word associates this file with the main document, so that the main document "knows" which fields are available.

4 When a message box states that your data source doesn't yet contain any records, click the Edit Data Source button. The process of typing records can take quite a while if you have a long mailing list. Luckily, you only have to do it once. (You can use this same data source with other main documents.)

5 Word displays the Data Form, which acts as an intermediary between you and the table that Word uses to store your data source. The Data Form contains a text box for each field. Type the data shown on the facing page for the first record. Press Tab to move to the next text box, and Shift+Tab to back up to a previous one. When you've finished typing the record, click the Add New button.

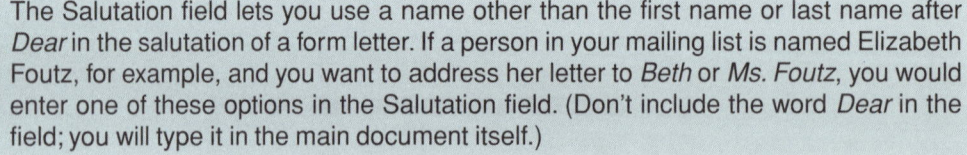

> ⓘ Make sure not to click the OK button at this point. If you do, Word closes the Data Form and displays the main document. To return to the Data Form, click the Edit Data Source button at the right end of the Mail Merge toolbar. (See the next lessons.)

6 Word empties the text boxes in the Data Form to let you enter another record. Enter three more records, using any addresses you wish. The current record number appears at the bottom of the Data Form. If you need to edit a record, use the red arrows to bring it into view. To delete a record, display it and then click the Delete button.

7 Click OK to close the Data Form, and go on to the next lesson without closing Word.

Mail Merge

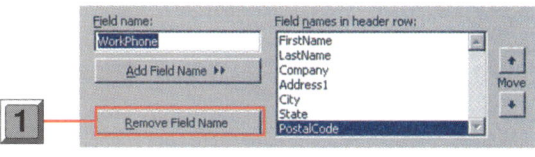

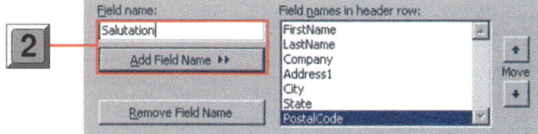

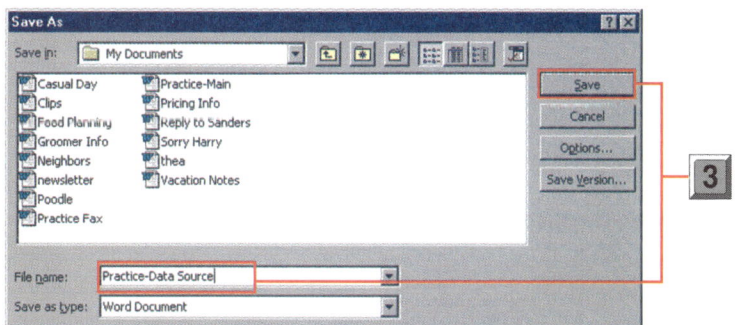

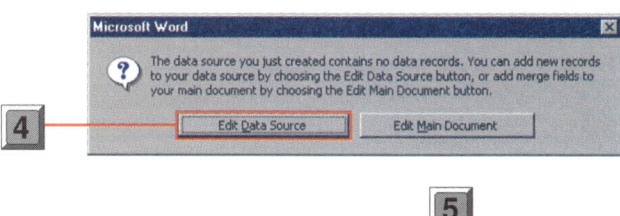

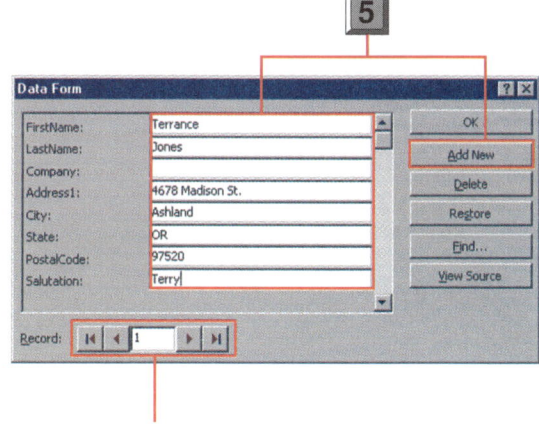

Use these buttons to
navigate between records

Mail Merge

❖ Completing the Main Document

This is the easiest part of performing a mail merge. If your main document is blank at this point, you need to both type (and format) the text and insert the merge codes. If the main document already contains text and formatting, you need only insert the codes.

1 After you closed the Data Form at the end of the previous lesson, Word displayed the main document. You should still have this document open on your screen.

2 The Mail Merge toolbar appears just under the Formatting toolbar. You'll use a few of its buttons in this lesson and the next.

3 Type the letterhead shown on the facing page, formatting it to suit your own tastes. Press Enter twice, choose Insert, Date and Time, click the third date format in the Date and Time dialog box, and click OK. Then press Enter two more times.

4 Click the Insert Merge Field button at the left end of the Mail Merge toolbar. Word displays a list of all of the fields in the data source that's attached to this main document. Click FirstName.

5 Word inserts the field in your document, surrounded by chevron brackets. Press the Spacebar once, and then click the Insert Merge Field button again. Choose LastName, and press Enter.

6 Continue using the Insert Merge Field button to insert the remaining fields in the address block, adding spaces and commas where necessary. Then press Enter twice, type **Dear**, press the Spacebar, insert the Salutation field, type a colon, and press Enter twice. (If the Office Assistant appears to help you with your letter, click its Close box to hide it.)

> ℹ️ If you need to delete a merge code, select it (so that the text appears white on a gray background) and then press the Delete key.

7 Type the text shown on the facing page for the body and closing of the letter.

8 Save the Practice-Main document, keep it open, and go on to the next lesson to run the merge.

> ℹ️ The next lesson describes how to perform a "standard" merge, in which Word merges every record in your data source into the main document, in whatever order you entered the records. However, Word also lets you merge a select group of records (only records for people who live in Berkeley, for example) instead of the entire data source. And it lets you sort records in a particular order before running the merge (perhaps by last name or zip code). If you want to sort or select records, click the Mail Merge button in the Mail Merge toolbar to display the Merge dialog box, and click the Query Options button. Define the sort and/or select options and click OK. Then click the Merge button to run the merge. Consult Word's help system to get more information about this.

Mail Merge

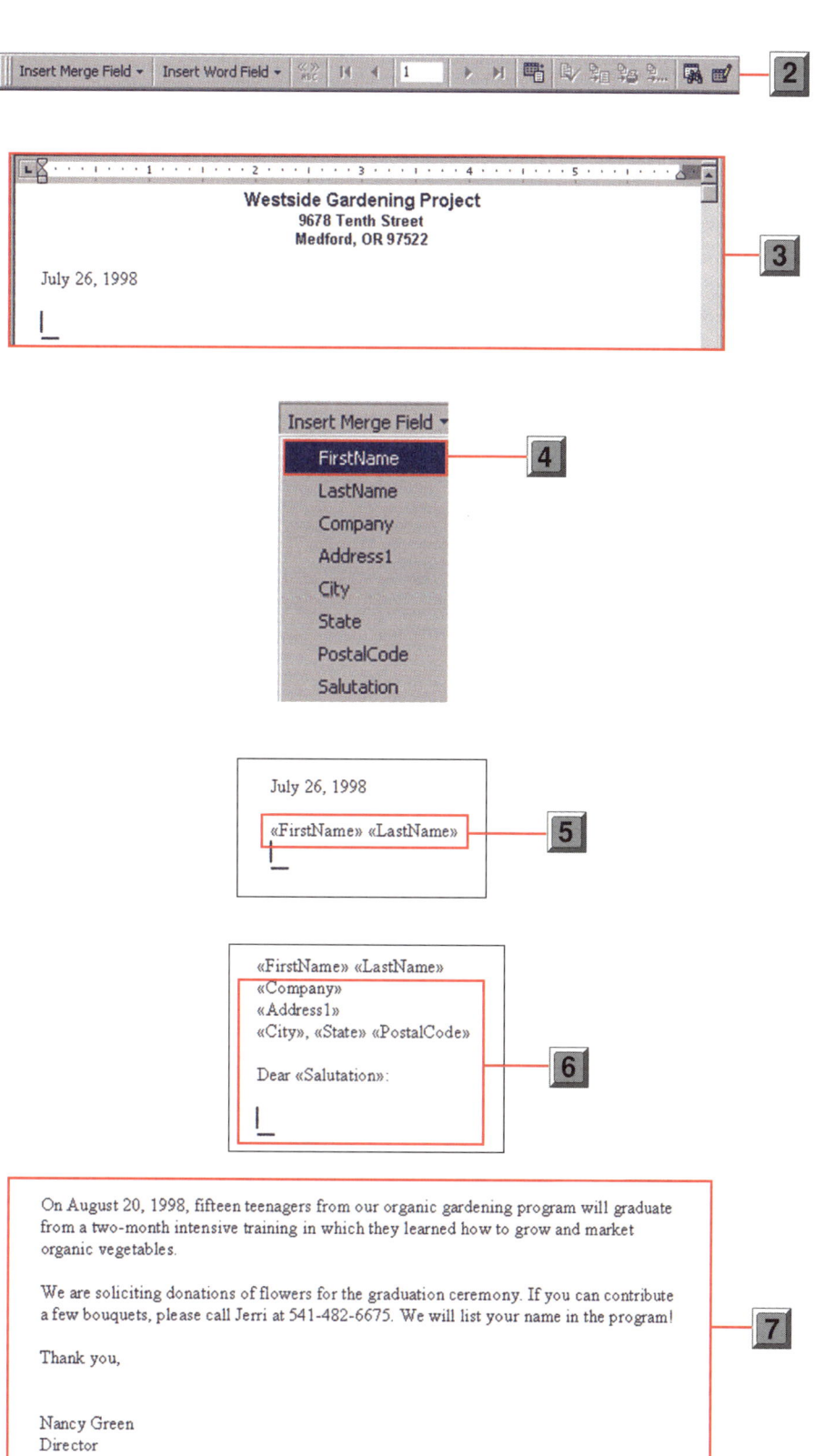

45 | Mail Merge

❖ Running the Merge

In this final phase of the merge process, Word merges the main document with the data source to produce a document called Form Letters1, which contains all of the merged letters.

1 Check that your main document, Practice-Main, is completed and open on your screen.

2 To confirm that you put the merge codes in the proper places and entered the information in the data source correctly, click the View Merged Data button on the Mail Merge toolbar. Word temporarily replaces the merge codes with the data from the first record of your data source. Because your first record doesn't contain a company name, Word automatically closed up what would be a blank line in the address block.

3 Use the Next Record button in the Mail Merge toolbar to review the data in the remaining three records.

> ℹ The easiest way to edit your data source in the future is to open it *through* the main document. First open the main document (File, Open) and then click the Edit Data Source button in the Mail Merge toolbar. Make your changes in the Data Form, and then click OK. Save the main document, and click the Yes button when Word asks if you want to save the data source attached to the main document.

4 When you're satisfied that everything looks good, click the View Merged Data button again to turn it off. Then click the Merge to New Document button on the Mail Merge toolbar to run the merge.

> ℹ The Merge to Printer button also runs a merge, but it sends the merged documents directly to the printer, without displaying them on your screen first.

5 Depending on the number of records in your data source, Word could take anywhere from a few seconds to several minutes to perform the merge. Since you only have four records, Word merges the data quickly. You should see the merged letters on your screen in a document named *Form Letters1*.

6 Scroll through the document to view the letters. The letters are separated with next page section breaks, so each one begins on a new page.

> ℹ If you discover problems in the Form Letters document, close it without saving, fix the problem where it originated—in the main document or the data source—and then run the merge again. Patching up the merged letters amounts to treating the symptoms and not the cause.

7 Click the Print button in the Standard toolbar to print your merged letters if you like, and then close Form Letters1 without saving it, close Practice-Main (if Word asks whether you want to save the attached data source, Practice-Data Source, click Yes), and exit from Word.

> ℹ To conserve hard disk space, you don't need to save merged letters. (The Form Letters document could be hundreds of pages long if you have a large data source.) Instead, you can keep track of the date you ran the merge and the names of the main document and the data source.

Mail Merge

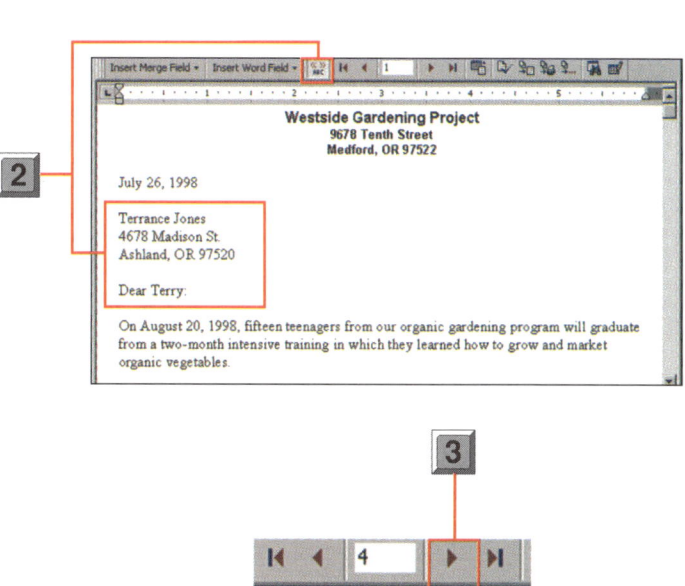

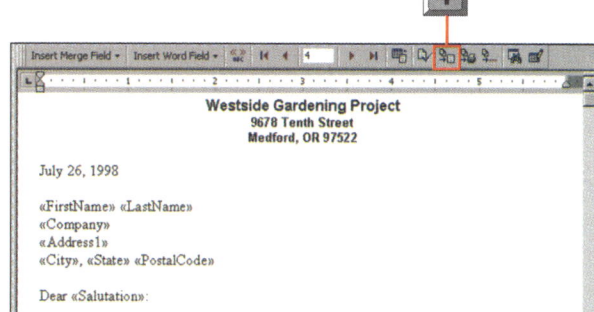

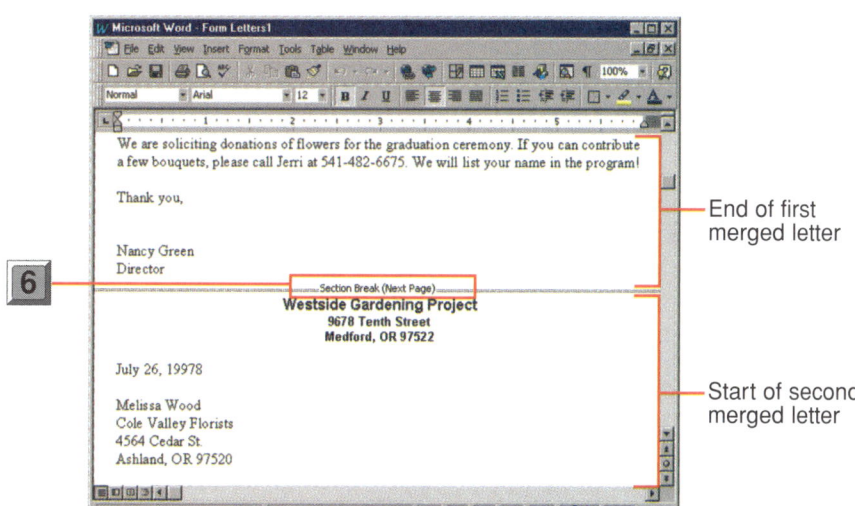

End of first
merged letter

Start of second
merged letter

《 》
ABC

**View
Merged
Data**

**Edit Data
Source**

**Merge to
New
Document**

Other titles available from
the BEGINNER'S GUIDE series:

TITLES	ISBN #	UPC #
Wordprocessing		
WordPerfect 6.0 for DOS / 6.1 for Windows	1-881023-80-X	7-25556-24717-3
MS Word 6.0 for Windows 3.1	1-881023-82-6	7-25556-24727-2
MS Word 7.0 for Windows 95	1-881023-92-3	7-25556-24728-9
MS Word 97	1-57671-013-0	7-25556-24729-6
Spreadsheet / Database		
MS Excel 5.0 for Windows 3.1	1-881023-83-4	7-25556-24752-4
MS Excel 7.0 for Windows 95	1-881023-93-1	7-25556-24753-1
MS Excel 97	1-57671-014-9	7-25556-24754-8
MS Access 7.0 for Windows 95	1-881023-88-5	7-25556-24791-3
Operating Systems		
MS Windows 3.1 / DOS 50.-6.2	1-881023-89-3	7-25556-24771-5
MS Windows 95	1-881023-90-7	7-25556-24772-2
Internet / Communications		
Netscape Communicator 4.0	1-57671-011-4	7-25556-24866-8
Finance / Home Finance		
Quicken Home Finance	1-881023-91-5	7-25556-24796-8
Office Suites		
MS Office for Windows 3.1	1-881023-87-7	7-25556-24781-4
MS Office for Windows 95	1-881023-94-X	7-25556-24782-1
MS Office 97	1-57671-012-2	7-25556-24783-8

To order, please contact us for the name
of your local distributor:

ACCESS Publishing
3015 112th Avenue NE Suite 205
Bellevue WA 98004-8001   USA
Telephone: 425.828.4223, Fax: 425.827.5895
e-mail: sales@access-pub.com